SCANDALS & CONSPIRACIES

ROBERT WILLIAMS

A SERIES OF TALKS FROM THE ESTEEMED PROFESSOR OF POLITICS, EXAMINING SOME OF THE 20TH CENTURY'S MOST SHOCKING AND SCANDALOUS COVER-UPS

CONTENTS

ACKNOWLEDGEMENTS

Writing and producing any book is a collaborative effort and I would like, once again, to thank my team at Collaborative Portfolio for their efforts on my behalf. Iain, Craig and Vikki all have skills I lack and I will always be grateful for their support.

But I want to dedicate this book to my wife, Jean, who first encouraged me to become a speaker on cruise ships and who has acted as principal supporter and critic for all my writing and speaking efforts. She gives meaning and purpose to my life and work and there are no words adequate to express my debt to her. I hope this book is one worthy of her.

Robert Williams

November 2014

1.
CRUISES AND CRUISE TALKS

If you have never been on a cruise, drop everything, go now! If money is a bit tight, remortgage the house, sell the children or (at least spend their inheritance). Do anything to experience the wonderful world of cruising. When I went on my first cruise only four years ago, I thought I would hate it but I absolutely loved it. There is something for everyone on a cruise and one striking feature of the better cruise lines is that they offer a selection of expert and celebrity speakers to keep you entertained and informed.

After our first cruise, my wife suggested I become a cruise speaker and, a month after applying; I got my first 'gig' in the Caribbean. Sheer heaven! My background as a political historian/consultant with expertise in corruption, scandals and political controversies proved to be a helpful preparation for delivering the kind of superior 'infotainment' demanded by leading cruise companies.

The talks I give on a variety of topics have proved exceptionally popular with cruise passengers who tell me they find them informative, amusing and stimulating. I invariably speak to packed audiences in large theatres on board giant cruise ships where the only passenger complaints are occasionally that they are unable to get seats. On several occasions, there have even been 'crowd control' incidents because passengers were blocking fire exits and stairways and the 'health and safety' officials were called in to restore order.

My talks have attracted glowing passenger reviews, for example;

'Standout entertainment... erudite, acerbic and self-deprecating.'
'The Professor was the star turn filling the Footlights

Theatre repeatedly.'
'One shining light was Professor Williams' talks...they
were just not to be missed.'
'Professor Williams' theories and explanations were the
talk of the ship.'
'The lectures were so good we couldn't bear to miss
any.'

I intend to continue with this new speaking career, but unfortunately, I have experienced some health problems and have reluctantly decided to cut back, at least temporarily, on cruise ship speaking. But the considerable public interest in my talks and writings have persuaded me to make a selection of my talks available in eBook form so that a wider audience can have access to my observations on important recent events and controversies.

The entertainment schedule on ships is packed and therefore talks are normally restricted to 45 minutes or an hour. Presenting them in written form also enables me to expand the talks, to give further examples and introduce anecdotes and facts that might be seen as little tangential to the topic but provide useful background and colour to my tales.

Although my talks cover a range of diverse topics, they share a similar approach. Their aim is to inform, entertain and stimulate the audience. I believe strongly that most official and accepted interpretations of important political and historical events and controversies are deeply and deliberately flawed and my talks seek to 'test' the official accounts and consider plausible alternatives.

The main purpose is not to persuade the listener or reader to accept my particular interpretation of such events, but rather to encourage them to reflect on and think critically about what the official accounts are claiming. In short, I encourage everyone to think for themselves and come to their own conclusions.

The talks selected for this eBook have attracted capacity audiences and very favourable comments from passengers aboard the numerous cruise ships on which I have been a Guest Entertainer and Lecturer including the Queen Elizabeth, Queen Victoria, Adonia, Arcadia, Azura, Oceana, Oriana, Ventura and the Black Watch. The topics include a mix of UK and US subjects to reflect interests on both sides of the Atlantic. I am always pleased to receive comments, suggestions, questions and speaking invitations from readers.

I spend a lot of time on the 'dark side' of public debates so it is hard not to become too cynical. One of my daughters once asked if I had always been a 'septic'. I replied, 'Do you mean sceptic?' And she responded with, 'No, I know what I mean.'

But it remains the fact that governments habitually and instinctively lie and cover-up their misdeeds. Politicians of all descriptions and ideologies are often absurd, corrupt and dishonest. Some would literally walk over their grandmothers for personal advancement or enrichment.

To help ward off depression about the political condition, each talk will be preceded by a story or joke about politics and corruption which may or may not have some relevance to the topic in question. Audiences and readers both need relief from the depressing activities of politicians!

You can learn more about me by going to my website: **www.robert-williams.co.uk** and you can contact me by email at **talks@robert-williams.co.uk**.

A newly elected British MP was being shown around Parliament by an official, but every time they passed another MP, the official murmured a sum of money; '£1000, £500, £2000'. The new MP asked what the official was referring to and was stunned when the official replied that the sum was the current bribe price of that particular MP.

The new MP was an innocent, idealistic man and was truly shocked. In a breaking, pleading voice, he asked, 'Are there no honest MPs, men and women of integrity motivated entirely by public service?'

'Oh yes, of course,' replied the official. 'Just a few. But they are very expensive!'

2.
MISADVENTURE OR MURDER?
THE DEATH OF DIANA, PRINCESS OF WALES

The untimely death of the British princess who became a global icon caused shock waves around the world. The British public reacted with an outpouring of grief which has no precedent. Like the Kennedy Assassination, many people claim to remember where they were when they heard the news. The flood of emotion took everyone, not least the Royal Family, by surprise and the apparent 'insensitivity' of the monarch in not rushing back to London provoked unusual and widespread criticism.

The Prime Minister, Tony Blair, allegedly helped persuade the royals that a different public response was required and Blair himself rose to the occasion with his apparently spontaneous - but really carefully scripted - speech to the effect that Diana was 'the People's Princess'. Blair proved to be in touch with public opinion at the time, but judgments of Diana remain contentious and depend in large part on how the break-up of her marriage to Prince Charles is viewed.

I should perhaps make it clear where I stand. I am not a

'Dianista', someone who ascribes almost saintly qualities to the late princess. But neither am I one of those who blame Diana for undermining the reputation of the Royal Family.

The Republican sentiment is undeveloped in the UK largely because of the exemplary conduct and standing of Queen Elizabeth, whose dedication and service are widely admired. Like many others, I am more of a 'Queenist' than a royalist and it remains to be seen how the reputation of the monarchy survives the passing of the present monarch and the accession of her son.

The wedding of William and Kate and the birth of their son, Prince George, both served as reminders of Diana's passing and speculation about the nature of her death continues unabated some 17 years later. In 2003, according to one opinion poll, almost half the UK population believed that there was some kind of 'cover-up' of the true circumstances of her death.

There has been a rash of conspiracy theories which set out a range of, sometimes bizarre, explanations of what 'really happened'. A chief advocate of these theories is Mohamed Al-Fayed, the father of Dodi who died alongside Diana.

Before assessing Al-Fayed's claims, I should perhaps make clear that I have a somewhat different view of the man than that expressed in the popular press. This is partly because I am a long-time supporter of Fulham Football Club and, for many years, Al-Fayed was our owner. So where others saw a 'dodgy' Egyptian businessman, I tended to see an altruistic benefactor!

But the understandable focus on the death of Diana has obscured the fact that Al-Fayed lost his eldest son in the crash and perhaps the depth of his grief may mitigate at least some of his wilder accusations.

It is, of course, difficult to pick a safe path through the different claims and judgments made about the circumstances of Diana's death but it is probably helpful to set out a brief cast of characters as well as a chronology of events to refresh our memories and provide reference points for future discussion.

CAST OF CHARACTERS

A Princess; Diana, Princess of Wales
A Playboy and Sometime Film Producer; Dodi Al-Fayed
A Businessman; Mohamed Al-Fayed
A Hotel Security Man and Driver; Henri Paul
Two Bodyguards; Kes Wingfield and Trevor Rees-Jones
A Policeman; Sir John Stevens, leader of Metropolitan Police investigation
A Judge; Lord Justice Scott Baker, chaired the Inquest
A Paparazzo; James Andanson

TIMELINE

30/08/97 -3.15pm
Diana and her then boyfriend, Dodi, arrive back from holiday together by private jet at a Paris airport where they are met by Henri Paul, deputy head and temporarily acting head of security at the Ritz Hotel. Paparazzi have been alerted to their arrival and are out in force. This irritates Dodi, who tells their chauffeur to 'lose them'. Their convoy of cars speeds into Paris and arrives at the Ritz hotel.

30/08/97 - 6pm
Dodi goes to nearby jewellers to pick up a ring he has ordered as a present for Diana. There has been much subsequent speculation as to whether this ring was intended as an engagement ring.

30/08/97 - 7pm
Diana and Dodi leave the Ritz Hotel and are driven to Dodi's apartment near the Arc de Triomphe by their chauffeur. They

have to enter at the rear of the apartments because of the paparazzi waiting for them at the front.

30/08/97 - 7.05pm
Henri Paul leaves the Ritz, telling colleagues to call him should the couple return, although he is expecting them to spend the night at Dodi's apartment.

30/08/97 - 9.30pm
Dodi and Diana's plan to eat at a restaurant close to his apartment is spoilt by a pack of paparazzi. They decide to return to the Ritz for dinner where they can get some privacy.

30/08/97 - 9.55pm
The couple return to the Ritz Hotel. They enter the restaurant, but again Diana seems distressed by intrusion of other diners and they decide to take their meal in a private suite at the hotel.

30/08/97 - 10.01pm
Henri Paul returns to the hotel and joins the two bodyguards, Kes Wingfield and Trevor Rees-Jones, in the hotel bar. Paul has two drinks, both Ricards - an aniseed flavour pastis. The bodyguards later testify that they believed he was drinking fruit juice.

30/08/97 - 11pm
Paul is seen at the front of the hotel talking with paparazzi and is reported as telling them that the couple will leave shortly from the front of the hotel.

30/08/97 - 11.37pm
Paul goes to the suite and speaks with Dodi and Diana, who inform him they are returning to Dodi's apartment for the night. Paul reports to the bodyguards that a decoy plan will be put in place to elude the paparazzi.

The vehicles which brought them from the airport will be brought to the front of the Ritz and will leave with the bodyguards. Meanwhile, Dodi and Diana will leave in another car to be driven by Paul from the back of the hotel. The bodyguards object to the lack of protection and it is agreed that one of the bodyguards, Rees-Jones, will travel with the couple.

Who devised this plan? Paul? Dodi? Diana? Mohamed Al-Fayed later gave evidence that he advised the couple to spend the night at the hotel.

31/08/97 - 12.20am

The decoy Mercedes pulls up and the couple leave with Henri Paul. But there are some paparazzi watching the rear and the decoy is unsuccessful. The Mercedes is pursued by a number of motorcycles and other vehicles.

31/08/97 - 12.25am

The Mercedes has a minor, glancing collision with a white Fiat Uno at the entrance to the Alma Tunnel. This collision is not publicly disclosed for some weeks. Paul subsequently loses control of the vehicle, which is travelling at some 65mph and, there being no safety barriers, crashes into the 13th pillar of the tunnel. Paul and Dodi are killed outright while Diana and Rees-Jones are seriously injured.

31/08/97 - 12.25am

The first paparazzi arrived at the scene of the accident. Among the first to arrive were the probably aptly named Romuald Rat and Nikolai Arsov!

31/08/97 - 12.26am

A French doctor, Dr Mailliez, drives in the opposite direction through the tunnel, sees the wreckage of the crash and stops and calls for emergency assistance.

31/08/97 - 12.28-32am
Police, fire and ambulance arrive at the crash scene. The police officers have great difficulty in cordoning off the crash scene from the increasing numbers of paparazzi, who are taking photographs inside the wrecked car. Seven paparazzi are arrested and removed from the tunnel.

31.08/97 - 1.25am
After almost an hour, the ambulance carrying Diana leaves for the hospital. She has suffered a cardiac arrest.

31/08/97 - 1.55am
The ambulance stops en route to the hospital while Diana is injected with adrenaline.

31/08/97 - 2.06am
The ambulance eventually arrives at the Pitie-Salpetriere hospital, some hour and 40 minutes after the crash.

31/08/97 - 2.06-4am
Medical staff work on trying to save Diana, but at 4am, she is pronounced dead.

The death of the Princess of Wales made news headlines across the world and set off a media frenzy. The arrest of the seven paparazzi immediately threw suspicion on the media as the cause of her demise. But the situation changed the next day when the autopsy results on Henri Paul were released. They showed that his blood alcohol readings were about three times the French drink driving limit.

The French standard is stricter than the British equivalent, and Paul was about twice the British standard. The conclusion was obvious; Diana had been killed by a drunk driver in the employ of Mohamed Al Fayed.

The autopsy results also revealed some other, very curious, results. Paul seemingly had an astonishingly high carbon monoxide reading of 20.7%. Speculation about the implications and veracity of this reading was to fuel conspiracy theories, as well as calling into question the accuracy of the blood alcohol readings.

While the Western media were almost unanimous in blaming Henri Paul for the crash, media elsewhere - especially in the Middle East and around the Islamic world - came to a very different conclusion: Diana had been murdered.

The 'hit' had been carried out by the secret service on behalf of the British government and the Royal family because the prospect of the mother of a future British king marrying a Muslim was simply unacceptable to the British establishment. Mohamed Al-Fayed picked up on this interpretation of events and identified a key role for Prince Philip as the mastermind behind what he saw as an assassination.

The investigation of the crash was complicated by the competing agendas of the different parties. Al-Fayed pressed for an inquest to open immediately, but numerous legal objections were lodged; not least that the French authorities should be allowed time and space to carry out their own investigations in their own way.

The result was that the British inquest led by Justice Scott Baker into the crash in 1997 did not open for another 11 years.

In 2008, the British inquest jury found by a majority verdict of 9-2 that Diana and Dodi were killed unlawfully due to the manner and speed of driving of the Mercedes and the following vehicles. The verdict also referred to Henri Paul's drink driving and the fact that none of the deceased were wearing seat belts.

But the inquest verdict did little to quench the speculation concerning the death of the princess. Those who favour the 'drunk driver' explanation have been keen to point out that

Al-Fayed shares responsibility for employing such an unreliable person.

Conspiracy theorists who believe in a conspiracy to murder have elaborated a variety of means and mechanisms by which the deed was accomplished. In some accounts, powerful strobe lights were shone in the driver's eyes to blind him. Others suggest that the Mercedes had been tampered with in a variety of ways, including disabling the seat belts.

Other accounts focus more on the mysterious white Fiat Uno which caused a collision with the Mercedes and which has never been definitively traced and identified. The finger of suspicion points at the security services - British and French - but it is in the nature of such organisations to admit nothing and to disclose less.

But you do not have to be a conspiracy theorist to be troubled by a number of as yet unresolved and unexplained features of what is officially described as a traffic accident. Nor is it paranoid to query whether evidence presented at the inquest is reliable and truthful. And there is nothing odd about asking why certain witnesses did not give evidence, or why certain questions were not asked.

It may be helpful to consider some of these loose ends before arriving at any conclusions about the death of Princess Diana.

TWENTY UNANSWERED QUESTIONS ABOUT THE DEATH OF DIANA

1. The Foreign and Commonwealth Office and the Secret Intelligence Service (MI6) both say they did not know Diana was in Paris. As the world's media seemed very clear where she was, are the official denials and claims of ignorance credible? And if they are not credible, why are these organisations dissembling? Do they have something to hide?

2. Where was Henri Paul between 7pm and 10pm? Despite allegedly extensive police investigations, nobody knows where he went or what he was doing. Was he meeting with his security service handlers as some conspiracy theorists allege? Or was he perhaps meeting some media and paparazzi contacts?

3. Was Henri Paul a drunk driver? On the CCTV at the Ritz Hotel, he shows no external signs of being under the influence. Would the bodyguards -Wingfield and Rees-Jones - have let Paul drive if they had any suspicion that he had been drinking heavily? Why did Sir John Stevens allegedly tell Paul's parents that he did not think their son was a drunk driver?

4. What are we to make of Paul's blood alcohol levels? Are the reported readings accurate, or is it possible that the samples were mishandled or even wrongly identified? At the Inquest, Lord Justice Scott Baker said, 'There are unsatisfactory aspects of the sampling and recording procedures,' and goes on to suggest that not only did the processes not meet UK standards, but indicated 'a lack of care at the very least'.

5. Were the correct blood samples analysed? Conspiracy

theorists argue that Paul's supposed blood samples actually belonged to another individual, and they point to the fact that the French doctors who carried out the tests refused both to attend the Inquest and to answer questions by video link. Given the handling of the samples, would Paul have been convicted of drink driving if he had survived the crash?

6. What about the extremely high carbon monoxide readings? Such readings are consistent with the individual concerned feeling very ill and even lapsing into unconsciousness. These remain a mystery and the Inquest experts could only conclude that the results were 'difficult to explain'.

7. Was Henri Paul simply a bad driver and was that the reason for the crash? Probably not; although not a professional chauffeur, he had been sent on anti-kidnapping and anti-terrorist evasion driving courses run by Mercedes in Stuttgart, and he had a lot of experience driving Mercedes vehicles. Experts testified that it was perfectly possible to drive through the Alma tunnel at Paul's speed - 65mph, according to estimations by the police.

8. What about the now notorious white Fiat Uno which police concluded had a minor collision with the Mercedes near the mouth of the Alma tunnel? Despite allegedly exhaustive searches, the French police said they could not trace it. Does that suggest that someone did not want it to be found? It seems the French search was concentrated in the Paris region and, when a very suspicious white Uno was located outside Paris by Al Fayed's detectives, they were then threatened with arrest for interfering in a police investigation.

9. What did the 17 CCTV cameras on the route to the Alma Tunnel reveal? Nothing, because they were either not aimed at the road or they were not working.

10. Why was the Alma Tunnel not searched more thoroughly and why was it reopened so quickly? It was not treated as a potential crime scene but as a straightforward traffic accident. The emphasis was on getting the traffic moving again rather than on a proper forensic examination of a crime scene.

11. Did one or more paparazzi manage to get in front of the Mercedes and help cause the crash by dazzling Henri Paul with their flash photography? Were even more powerful lights shone in the eyes of the driver by persons unknown? Only one paparazzo gave evidence at the Inquest and he denied doing this but, as Mandy Rice-Davies once observed in a different context, 'he would, wouldn't he?'

12. Why did it take so long - nearly two hours - to get Diana to hospital? The so-called 'golden hour' immediately after sudden trauma is critical to determining outcomes for patients. Could Diana have been saved if she had been delivered to a hospital with greater haste? American practice is to 'scoop and run' and this is informed by the conviction that only hospitals have the appropriate doctors, equipment and facilities to save the most seriously injured.

13. Why was Diana not taken to the nearest hospital? Why was she not evacuated by helicopter from the mouth of the tunnel? The answers seem to be that only certain hospitals had the right experience and equipment to receive her, and that French emergency practice is to 'stay and play'; in other words, to stabilise and give initial treatment at the scene. The success of this approach depends on the ability of attending doctors or paramedics to accurately identify and assess the seriousness of internal injuries outside of a hospital setting. It seems likely that Diana would have died anyway, but would she at least have had a better chance if rushed to hospital?

14. Why was Diana's body embalmed? On which person's

order or authority? The Inquest failed to establish this but what role, if any, did her former husband, Prince Charles, play? One consequence of the decision to embalm is that it made it impossible to determine whether or not Diana was pregnant.

15. Did Henri Paul work for one or more intelligence services? His role in one of the world's leading hotels means he was well placed to report on the activities of the rich and powerful. If he did not work for any security service, how can we account for his sizeable savings of £170,000 distributed around 15 different bank accounts? Did he tip off one or more of the paparazzi about the route back to Dodi's apartment for financial reward?

16. What role, if any did James Andanson play? Andanson (aka Jean-Paul Gonin) was known as the 'king of the paparazzi' and a very successful photo journalist with a millionaire lifestyle. He was very pro-British and had followed Diana and Dodi around that summer, even chartering helicopters and boats to get close to them. It is said he would do anything to get the 'killer' photograph. Andanson denied being in Paris that evening, but he did own a white Fiat Uno of the right age at the time of the crash. He told the police he had got rid of it before the crash but, in fact, it was sold shortly thereafter, repaired and resprayed a different colour. Andanson was described by Lord Justice Scott Baker at the Inquest as a 'proven liar'.

17. Why wasn't Andanson called to give evidence at the Inquest? Because the Inquest took place in 2008, some eleven years after the crash and Andanson died in May 2000. He was found dead in a burnt-out car and the official verdict was suicide, though there was no obvious motive. But the first responders, a fire fighter and police officer, have suggested that he had a bullet hole in his skull! So did he set himself on

fire and then shoot himself? Or did he shoot himself and then set himself on fire?

18. If Andanson was murdered, who was responsible and why? Was it to 'keep him quiet'? What story did he have to tell? Was it revenge? Why was Andanson's photo agency burgled by armed robbers on the night after the crash? I believe a professional hit is available for around £10,000; well within the budgets of many people who might blame Andanson for the death of a loved one or who were concerned to prevent the truth emerging.

19. Were Diana and Dodi about to announce their engagement? Dodi went to a jewellery store that afternoon to pick up a ring for Diana and the Princess had told friends she had a big announcement to make which would shock the world. Was she killed to stop that announcement being made?

20. If Diana intended to marry a Muslim, how would that be viewed by the government and the Royal Family? Is that a sufficient motive for murder?

It is, of course, possible to ask further questions, but the chances of finding definitive answers to the twenty questions already identified seem small.

Despite the millions spent by the French authorities, the money spent by Al Fayed's own investigations and the ten million pounds or so spent by Lord Stevens' police investigations and Lord Scott Baker's Inquest, it appears that, in many respects, the death of Diana remains a mystery.

But I will offer my own interpretation of the available evidence and raise some additional issues for readers' consideration.

MURDER OR MISADVENTURE?

Al-Fayed will go to his grave believing that his son was killed by the intervention of a third party. He believes in a major conspiracy to murder Dodi and Diana and nothing is likely to change his mind. In Al-Fayed's mind, Prince Philip was the criminal mastermind and was directing the activities of the security services, and it was they who carried out the crime.

This suggests an unusual and improbable understanding of the chain of authority in British government, but we should always remember that even the paranoid sometimes have enemies. Former Prime Minister Harold Wilson was accused of paranoia when he alleged that MI5 were plotting to overthrow him because they believed he was a Soviet agent!

But it was later revealed by Peter Wright of Spycatcher notoriety that a number of MI5 officers did actually plot against Wilson. There really was a meeting of the 'great and the good' to plot a coup d'etat.

But just because something might be true does not make it plausible or probable. It is a large step to believe in a master plan orchestrated by the security services under the direction of the Royal Family.

There is little doubt that the prospect of Diana marrying Dodi would have appalled the Royal Family and the government but it is a strange kind of plot that requires the victim not to wear a safety belt. If Diana had fastened her belt, she would have survived the crash. The only evidence for a possible marriage comes from the claims of Mohamed Al-Fayed. Diana's friends and sister dispute this.

While I accept it is no accident or oversight that there is no statue of Diana -she has been airbrushed from the royal memory - and that Prince Charles was probably relieved that his ex-wife would no longer distract public attention from himself and his new consort, it is still a leap to imagine a conspiracy to murder. And if you wanted to run a large, heavy Mercedes saloon off the road, you would hardly choose to do it with a light, flimsy Fiat Uno.

But if it wasn't murder, was it manslaughter by negligence?
Was it criminal negligence by the French and British authorities to fail to protect the mother of our future king from intrusive, aggressive paparazzi?

Was the crash caused by the paparazzi - or one paparazzo in particular, James Andanson?

Why did Paul choose the particular and not most direct route to Dodi's apartment? Had he tipped off one or more photographers so they could lie in wait? This seems more plausible than a security service operation.

In 2003 almost half of the British public believed there was some sort of cover-up in the death of Diana. Even after the lengthy 2008 Inquest, polls suggest that between a quarter and a third still believe in a conspiracy and most of those polled have never heard of James Andanson and his white Fiat Uno.

I would like to end this topic by raising some different questions;

Are some cover-ups justifiable?

Perhaps in order to protect the reputations of the deceased or to spare the feelings of their nearest and dearest? If Diana was pregnant at the time of her death, did William and Harry need to know?

Do I believe there was a conspiracy to murder Diana and Dodi?

No.

Do I think the French and British authorities - police, security and medical services - were really determined to avoid any blame?

Yes.

Was Andanson implicated in the crash?

Quite possibly.

Can you have a cover-up without really having a crime?

Yes. And that it what I think happened in the tragic case of the death of Diana, Princess of Wales.

The Prosecutor in a serious criminal trial confronts a witness in court and says, 'Isn't it true that you accepted £20,000 to fix this trial?'

The witness makes no reply and simply stares at the Judge. The Prosecutor repeats the question again and again, each time more forcibly, but still the witness continues to look at the Judge and remains silent. Eventually, the Judge leans forward and tells the witness that when the Prosecutor asks a question, the witness has to answer it.

The witness looks a little flustered and says, 'Oh, I'm so sorry Your Honour, I thought the Prosecutor was talking to you!'

3.
A VERY BRITISH SCANDAL
THE PROFUMO AFFAIR

The Profumo scandal is the scandal to end all scandals. It has everything any scandal lover would want. It is a tale of sex and violence, of spying and lying, of conspiracy and frame-ups, and of power and hypocrisy. It was a scandal which made household names of Christine Keeler and Mandy Rice-Davies. More importantly, it had major political consequences and it not only forced a sensational ministerial resignation, but contributed to the downfall of a Prime Minister - and arguably even influenced the outcome of the 1964 General Election.

But because it all happened a long time ago in the early 1960s, it is necessary to establish a little context and a frame of reference before we get into telling the story. The social and political world of the early 1960s was very different from the modern world and it is important to understand what has changed, what has stayed the same and who's who.

CAST OF CHARACTERS

A Government Minister; John Profumo
A Society Osteopath and Artist; Stephen Ward
A Diplomat and Spy; Yegeny(Eugene) Ivanov
A Party Girl; Christine Keeler
Another Party Girl; Mandy Rice-Davies
An Aristocrat; 3rd Lord Astor
Two Criminals; Lucky Gordon and Johnny Edgecombe
A Prime Minister; Harold Macmillan
A Judge; Lord Denning

CONTEXT AND BACKGROUND

In the late 1950s and early 1960s, British society was socially and politically conservative with a large and small 'c'. Social position was identified by your class identity, where you went to school or university and even by military service to your country. Certain regiments in the army, for example the Guards regiments, attracted social prestige while others were regarded less favourably.

By 1963 the Conservative Party had been in office for twelve years and the premiership had been passed from Churchill to Eden to Macmillan. The opposition Labour Party was in disarray and 'Supermac', as Macmillan became known, seemed to have a firm grip on the support of the British public.

During this period what might be called ordinary people or the common folk were expected to 'know their place'. Britain was run by 'the Establishment', by the 'Old Boy' network and the old school, university or regimental tie provided access and preferential treatment. In economic terms, Britain had 'never had it so good' so there was no need to change anything. The people in charge of the government 'knew best' what was good for the workers, so there was no need for revolt or revolution. All that was needed to keep faith with the 'ruling class'.

Our 'betters' knew what was good for us and, more particularly, what was bad for us. Thus we had censorship of books, in the theatre and, through 'D' notices, the press. This was a time when there was no women's liberation, no gay liberation, no contraceptive pills and no divorce liberalisation. Journalists were imprisoned for not revealing their sources, and plays and even books were banned.

Most famously, there was a prosecution of Lawrence's Lady Chatterley's Lover for obscenity. The prosecutor in the case, Mervyn Griffith-Jones, later appeared as the prosecutor and tormentor of Stephen Ward, but his social position and attitudes can be measured by him asking the jury whether the novel, Lady Chatterley's Lover, was one you would 'wish your wife and servants to read'. It simply did not occur to him that some members of the jury might not have servants!

In the political realm, the Cold War between the Western powers and the Soviet Union was at its most intense. The Berlin Wall dividing the city was built in 1961 and, in the Cuban Missile Crisis of the following year, the world stood on the brink of nuclear annihilation. Britain was beset by espionage scandals; Gordon Lonsdale and the Portland spy ring, William Vassall, George Blake and then Kim Philby all became household names.

The American government eventually became extremely sceptical about the British government's ability to keep any secrets. One of the reasons that people like Philby got away with years of damaging espionage is that they were regarded as 'one of us', as 'sound chaps' who had shared similar life experiences with those who ultimately had to investigate them.

They were above suspicion because if a gentleman gives his word that he is not a spy and has committed no misconduct, then another gentleman just has to believe him. Trust was established by shared backgrounds, similar accents and shared values. Some people thus became truly 'above suspicion'.

The present British cabinet is also full of millionaires so perhaps little changes and because the Prime Minister's wife now has the 4th Lord Astor as her step-father, there is a connection to the principals in the Profumo affair. But although we now have a coalition government with Cameron and Clegg, or shampoo and conditioner as I like to think of them, the men of Macmillan's Cabinet were more aristocratic, men of wider experience and of a generation that had fought - sometimes with great distinction - in the World Wars. Macmillan himself was wounded five times in World War One.

It might be thought by anyone under 65 that life in the early 1960s was rather dull; only two television channels and they were in black and white; no multi channel entertainment; no 24/7 news channels; no computers; no Internet; no mobile phones; no social media; no Facebook or Twitter. People made their own entertainment and, of course, some people made rather more than others. So to set the scene for the first episode in what became the Profumo scandal, I want to take you back to a hot, steamy July night in 1961.

Perhaps you could imagine for a moment that you are John (Jack) Profumo. You are a powerful rising politician in your mid-forties and a Minister of the Crown, Minister for War no less at a time when Britain could afford aircraft carriers with real planes on them. Who knows, you might one day become Foreign Secretary; after all, Macmillan likes you.

Better still, you are very rich through inherited wealth. Your family own the major share of the Provident Insurance Company. You had a 'good war', rising to the rank of Brigadier. Are you with me so far? This is one lucky man. You do have something of a reputation as a 'ladies man' but even better, you have the good fortune to be married to Valerie Hobson, one of Britain's most famous and attractive film stars.

One of your closest friends is Bill Astor (Lord Astor to you and I, reader) of the famous Anglo-American Waldorf-Astor family. His mother was the fearsome Nancy Astor, the first woman to take her seat as an MP in the House of Commons. Nancy was just a tad right-wing, and in the 1930s she used to hold social events at her home at Cliveden House for a variety of appeasers and other far right pro-German notables. During World War Two, she became known in Parliament as the Member for Berlin!

Jack has been invited by Bill to an exclusive dinner party at Cliveden House. Among the other house guests are the President of Pakistan, Ayub Khan, Lord Mountbatten and Nubar Gulbenkian and, naturally, they dressed formally for dinner - doesn't everyone? But it was a hot, sultry night and Profumo, Khan and Astor went outside for some fresh air and to smoke their cigars. They heard noise and laughter coming from the swimming pool terrace and their curiosity led them in that direction.

A man called Stephen Ward had both the use of a cottage on the Cliveden Estate and permission to use the pool for £1 a year in exchange for treating Astor's bad back. So, on this fateful evening, there were actually two parties going on at Cliveden. One involved the great and the good, the other the fun lovers and uninhibited - namely, Ward and his friends. When the group of friends from the posh party reached the pool, Profumo stopped dead in his tracks.

You have seen somebody who will change your life forever, someone who will cause you and those you love untold misery. Someone who will destroy your glittering career and bring down the government you are so proud to serve.

A beautiful young woman with auburn hair emerges naked from the swimming pool right in front of you. You stand stock still. Your heart is pounding, your mouth is suddenly dry and you find it hard to speak.

Before you can gather your wits, someone says, 'That's

Christine Keeler'. Then your wife appears alongside you and the vision slips back into the water. But it is too late; you are bewitched, you are lost. It will all end in tears.

Okay, you can stop imagining you are Jack Profumo now!

Within 24 hours, Profumo has acquired her telephone number - she was currently staying at Ward's flat - cavorted with her in the swimming pool at a another party the following day, and escorted her on a tour of Cliveden House. There, he made physical advances to her, and their affair began in earnest.

Given some of the complexity of this scandal, it may again be useful to set out a brief timeline of events before proceeding to any analysis and evaluation of their meaning and importance.

TIMELINE

November 1959
Ward meets Keeler at Murray's Club in Soho.

March 1960
Ivanov arrives as Naval Attaché at Soviet Embassy.

January 1961
Sir Colin Coote, Daily Telegraph Editor and former MI5, introduces Ward to Ivanov.

8th June 1961
Ward first contacted by MI5 about Ivanov.

8th/9th July 1961
The Cliveden Parties.

July/August 1961
Profumo's affair with Keeler.

October 1961
Ward and Keeler meet Lucky Gordon.

May 1962
MI5 has further contact with Ward.

October 1962
Mandy Rice-Davies moves into Wimpole Mews flat with Keeler and Ward after a row with her lover, Peter Rachman.

November 1962
Rachman dies after heart attack and Rice-Davies attempts suicide. Her parents also move into Ward's flat while she recovers.

14th December 1962

Johnny Edgecombe, one of Keeler's past boyfriends, comes looking for her but Mandy Rice-Davies will not open the door to him because Keeler is frightened of him. Edgecombe starts shooting at the doors and windows, then rushes off and is subsequently arrested.

26th January 1963

Keeler tells police she had sex with Profumo.

14th March 1963

Edgecombe goes on trial but the principal witness, Keeler, fails to appear. Private Eye insinuates that Profumo has arranged for her disappearance.

21st March 1963

Labour MPs George Wigg, Richard Crossman and Barbara Castle raise questions in the House of Commons about 'the Minister and the missing model'.

22nd March 1963

Profumo meets five ministerial colleagues in the early hours of the morning to draft a personal statement which is delivered to the silent House of Commons that afternoon. Profumo is flanked by the Prime Minister and Attorney General. He denies all allegations of impropriety and threatens to sue anyone who repeats such allegations outside the protection of parliamentary privilege.

26th March 1963

Ward meets openly with George Wigg in House of Commons tea room.

27th March 1963

Home Secretary (Sir Henry Brooke) is suspicious of Ward and calls the Director of MI5 (Roger Hollis) and the

Commissioner of the Metropolitan Police (Sir Joseph Simpson) to a meeting and asks if Ward can be charged with something. Hollis and Simpson are doubtful.

April 1st 1963
Investigation of Ward begins. 140 potential witnesses are interviewed, Ward's phone is tapped and his home and surgery are put under surveillance.

18th April 1963
Keeler is assaulted by John Hamilton-Marshall - but she accuses Lucky Gordon.

19th May 1963
Ward complains to Home Secretary that he is being ruined by police investigation.

20th May 1963
Ward copies his letter to all newspaper editors, but they are too frightened to publish. Ward writes to Harold Wilson telling him that Profumo has been lying.

4th June 1963
Profumo resigns.

7th June 1963
Lucky Gordon convicted of assaulting Keeler and receives a three year sentence.

8th June 1963
Ward is arrested. He is denied bail.

9th June 1963
A parliamentary debate is held, where Ward is referred to as a Soviet agent and Keeler and Rice-Davies are termed 'prostitutes' and 'harlots'.

28th June 1963

Ward's committal proceedings where Rice-Davies gives her famous 'he would, wouldn't he' answer.

22nd July 1963

Ward's trial begins. He faces 5 charges.

30th July, 9am, 1963

The Court of Criminal Appeal overturns the jury's verdict in the Lucky Gordon assault case. The Chief Justice orders its decision to be hand-delivered to the Old Bailey.

30th July, 10.30am, 1963

The prosecution tells the jury of the Court of Appeal's decision and states that despite Gordon's acquittal, Keeler's evidence might be completely truthful. The Judge says in summing up that because Ward has been abandoned by his 'friends', it could mean it is less likely he is telling the truth.

Later that evening, Ward apparently attempts suicide.

31st July 1963

The Judge refuses to adjourn trial. The jury acquits Ward on three charges but convicts him on two.

3rd August 1963

Ward dies in hospital.

25th September 1963

Lord Denning's Report is published.

9th October 1963

Harold Macmillan resigns as Prime Minister.

6th December 1963

Keeler is sentenced to nine months in prison for committing perjury at Gordon's trial.

15th October 1964
Labour wins the General Election by four seats.

EXPLAINING THE PROFUMO AFFAIR

When commentators try to explain the dynamics of a political scandal, they often speak of the search for a 'smoking gun'. By this, they generally mean the one piece of evidence or event which defines the scandal in the public mind. The Profumo affair is unusual in that the defining event involved an actual 'smoking gun' and not just a metaphor.

When an angry Johnny Edgecombe started firing his gun at Ward's flat in December 1962 while Keeler and Rice-Davies cowered inside, it guaranteed extensive and intensive police and media attention and interest. Gun fire was relatively rare in London in the early 1960s; in such an upmarket location, it was unheard of.

The police wanted to know all about the occupants, their lifestyles, their means of support, and their connections with others - and so did the media. Who were these beautiful young women? What was their connection to West Indian criminals and dope users? Who was this Ward character in whose flat they were staying? Who were his friends?

Jack Profumo's dalliance with Christine Keeler had ended in the autumn of the previous year. He had apparently proposed setting up Keeler in her own flat so he could 'visit' her more easily and without others knowing, but Keeler had declined. He probably thought his illicit relationship with her was just a pleasant interlude but, to Profumo's loss, the Edgecombe shooting thrust Keeler and her circle into the public arena.

Who were Christine Keeler and Mandy Rice-Davies?

They were young women, very young in Mandy's case,

who had come to London to seek fame, fortune and excitement. Mandy had come to London as a 16 year old and managed to find some work as a model. She was Miss Austin in the 1960 motor show and was taking drama lessons in the hope of becoming an actress. Keeler had got a job as a showgirl in a nightclub and, after meeting Rice-Davies in a shop, she suggested that Rice-Davies join her at the club. Mandy duly got a job there as a dancer.

It was at the nightclub that first Keeler and then Rice-Davies met Stephen Ward. Both Keeler and Rice-Davies acquired a series of rich boyfriends, some through Ward and others through their work at the nightclub. I refer to them as party girls in my cast of characters, but the popular press and many MPs called them 'harlots' and 'prostitutes', which I think is inaccurate and unfair. They may have been 'good time girls' or 'gold diggers', to use the deprecating and sexist language of the period, but they did not merit the epithets hurled at them by politicians and the press.

When Keeler met Profumo at Cliveden, she was 19 years old. She stayed at Ward's flat from time to time but their relationship seems to have been largely platonic. Keeler had briefly been the mistress of the notorious slum landlord, Peter Rachman, and was replaced in that role by Mandy Rice-Davies. Mandy seems to have been genuinely fond of Rachman, who was apparently very charming if you were not one of his tenants! In any event, he paid her £80 a week, which, in the early 1960s, was many times the average wage.

But Mandy had a row with Rachman and Stephen Ward allowed her to stay at his flat while a reconciliation was negotiated. That explains why she was there when Edgecombe, a jealous former of boyfriend of Keeler's, came calling with his handgun. Edgecombe was further agitated because Keeler was threatening to testify against him for his assault on another of her former boyfriends, Lucky Gordon.

To Mandy's distress, Rachman died suddenly and she attempted suicide. Ward then found himself putting up

Mandy's parents as well in his not very large flat while they nursed their daughter back to health.

So who was this knight in shining armour, Stephen Ward?

Stephen Ward was the son of a clergyman who, by 1961, had become a successful and fashionable London osteopath. If you had a bad back, Ward was the man everyone who was anyone went to for treatment. The roll call of his patients is like an excerpt from Who's Who in that he treated politicians, film stars and members of the Royal Family.

Among his patients were Gandhi, Winston Churchill, Lord Astor and Paul Getty. The film stars included Danny Kaye, Ava Gardner and Douglas Fairbanks Jr. He had also treated the Duke of Edinburgh, the Duke of Kent and Lord Snowdon. In short, he was a high society osteopath.

But Ward had other talents and, in particular, he had real skill and talent as an artist. Many of the famous people he treated also sat for him to be sketched or painted. The Editor of the Daily Telegraph invited him to cover the trial of Adolf Eichmann in Israel and provide drawings from the court. Some of Ward's work can now be found in the National Portrait Gallery.

When he wasn't mending bad backs or sketching, Stephen Ward enjoyed the company of young, attractive women. Some of these women, like Keeler, stayed with him from time to time, though their relationship is hard to describe. Keeler once said that 'Ward filled a daddy-shaped vacuum in her life'.

Ward enjoyed a good party where he could invite any number of his famous friends, and there would always be pretty girls there. Regulars at his flat included people like Charles Clore, the property tycoon, Emile Savundra, the crooked insurance tycoon, and Ernest Marples, Conservative Minister of Transport.

We will examine in some detail the later attempts to prosecute Ward for a variety of sex-related offences but, for now, I would like to suggest that he seemed to see himself as a latter-day Professor Higgins from Pygmalion/ My Fair

Lady. A man of the world who got pleasure from taking 'ordinary' girls and introducing them to the world of the great and the good and who loved to see one of his protégés make the transition to consorts or even wives of the famous and well bred.

He enjoyed mixing in 'high society', but he also enjoyed 'low society'. After a weekend at Cliveden, he might find himself back in London at a West Indian club in Notting Hill in the early hours. From time to time, he used prostitutes, but seemed to regard it as nothing unusual. He thought there was a great deal of British hypocrisy about sex and he was not going to allow it to restrict his activities.

It is sometimes wrongly alleged that Ward simply held 'sex parties' and reference is sometimes made to the use of a two-way mirror for his alleged voyeuristic activities. But the mirror in question was installed in a London flat before Ward occupied it. It had been installed, not by Ward, but by Peter Rachman.

If you wanted to attend a London sex party in the early 1960s, you would have been better advised to go to one of those hosted by a real prostitute, Mariella Novotny, whose parties were legendary. She specialised in sado-masochistic punishments and she is reported to have once said that there were so many MPs receiving her punishments that they ought to make her the Chief Whip!

WAS JACK PROFUMO A SECURITY RISK?

When Profumo entered into his affair with Christine Keeler in the summer of 1961, he was not fully aware of Keeler's wider social circle. In particular, when Keeler returned to London from the Cliveden party, she was driven not by Ward but by one Yegeny Ivanov, who was generally known as Eugene to his British friends. There is much debate in the literature on the Profumo affair as to the Keeler/Ivanov relationship. Some suggest an ongoing affair, others a single casual sexual encounter, while still others insist it was a platonic relationship. I favour the single sexual encounter.

But all commentators agree that Ivanov was a spy using diplomatic cover. He met Ward at a lunch at the Daily Telegraph for military attaches. The Editor, Sir Colin Coote, was an ex-MI5 man himself and under no illusions as to what the real activities of many attaches in London were. Ward had expressed to Coote a wish to sketch the members of the Soviet politburo and it was thought that Ivanov may be able to facilitate this. In any event, Ward and Ivanov became friends and he was a regular visitor to Ward's flat.

The security services were well aware of Ivanov and they knew all about his visits to Ward. It seems MI5 had earlier suggested that Profumo be warned off visiting Ward's flat, not because they were aware of the Keeler affair, but because of the chances of meeting Ivanov. MI5 were interested in talking to Ward about Ivanov, partly to explore the prospects of 'turning' him, but perhaps also to consider a possible role as a conduit to the Soviet authorities at a time of intense East-West tension over Cuba.

MI5 knew that Ivanov was a regular visitor to Ward's flat - and they also knew that Profumo was too. The married War Minister appeared to be meeting with a very young woman - less than half his age - at the home of a third party, and that young woman seemed also to be involved with a known Soviet spy in the same flat.

It seems that Ward volunteered his services as a 'go-between' and would report back on anything interesting that was discussed. The possibility, the seed, then seemed to lodge in some security minds that, in being so keen to help, Ward might conceivably be working for the other side - the Soviet Union.

At the same time, there was a very interesting American parallel, in that while one of our Ministers was apparently sharing a mistress with a Soviet spy, the American president, John F. Kennedy, was sharing a mistress - one Judith EXNER - with the Chicago mafia boss, Sam Giancana!

And closer to home, Macmillan's wife, Dorothy, enjoyed a 30-year long affair with the bisexual Lord Boothby, who was simultaneously involved with the notorious Kray brothers. Some fine examples of model family life were being offered by our 'ruling classes'!

So were there any security implications? Was Keeler getting secret information from Ivanov to give to Ward? Was she getting secret information from Profumo to give to Ivanov or Ward? What did Keeler know or understand about military matters? Very little! In any event, some weeks after he started seeing Keeler, Profumo was warned by the Cabinet secretary to stay away from Ward's flat and social circle because of the likely presence of Ivanov.

Profumo's sexual encounters with Keeler had taken place mostly at Ward's flat, sometimes in a borrowed car and, on at least one occasion, at his family home, which Keeler was able to describe in some detail. And once he was warned off Ward's flat and Keeler refused to allow him to 'set her up' in her own flat, the 'romance' was doomed.

Who was told what and when about Profumo is difficult to determine with any great accuracy but, after the shooting incident, it seems that Macmillan asked the Cabinet Secretary and the Attorney-General, Sir John Hobson, to question Profumo. Hobson was a friend of Profumo's; they had attended the same school, gone to the same Oxford college and served in the same regiment in the army. This was not a hostile interview!

Profumo's strategy was to deny everything and use his wealth to threaten libel proceedings against anyone who dared impugn his reputation. The British press were, with the odd honourable exception, easily cowed, though some foreign press and magazines did run some of the rumours. Profumo sought the issue of a 'D' notice to ban all reporting of his alleged relationship but the Attorney General declined. So Profumo then asked the Attorney-General to consider prosecuting Keeler for attempted blackmail. He declined to do so.

There had been communication between Profumo's lawyers and those of Keeler. She was feeling hounded by the press and the police and decided to remove herself to Spain to allow time for the scandal to cool down but, as her lawyer pointed out, she had no funds to support herself while abroad.

Profumo seemed unaware that Keeler had spoken to a number of people about her affair with him and this information eventually reached the MP George Wigg, who was able to ask questions in the House of Commons using the protection of parliamentary privilege. There was no chance of Profumo being able to gag him.

Profumo also seemed to have forgotten that he had written several notes to Keeler which were 'affectionate' in character, and was unaware that Keeler had retained these notes and had shared them with at least one newspaper. The newspaper was too frightened to publish them. Ward also spoke to Wigg and wrote to Harold Wilson.

Eventually, Profumo was told he had to make a personal statement in the House of Commons to try finally to quash the rumours circulating about him. He agreed and the statement was heard, by tradition, in complete silence. He denied any improper relationship with Keeler, but cleverly tried to focus attention on his denial of assisting Keeler's flight to Spain.

But as more and more people learned what had really happened - friends of Ward, politicians and newspaper people - it became clear that the rumours were multiplying rather than going away.

So on the 4th of June, 1963, Jack Profumo tended his resignation as a Minister and as an MP. He apologised to Macmillan for deceiving him and retired immediately from public life. His own son said that his father never apologised for his behaviour or even spoke about the scandal, though it was later claimed that Profumo had lied to 'protect his wife'.

The Prime Minister asked Lord Denning to conduct an inquiry to see whether national security had been compromised. Denning was a distinguished jurist but not exactly a 'man of the world.' As we shall see later, he interpreted his brief quite widely and felt able, without any authority to do so, to assure witnesses that their evidence to him would remain secret in perpetuity!

Meanwhile, the Home Secretary, Henry Brooke, called a meeting with the head of MI5 and the commissioner of the Metropolitan Police to see if there were any security or other charges that could be brought against Stephen Ward. MI5 said they were not interested in Ward, so Brooke encouraged the police to see if they could find any grounds for any prosecution of this 'bounder' Ward, who had somehow been instrumental in bringing down a fine chap like Profumo.

In a normal police investigation, the police investigate a crime and then see if they can track the culprit but, in Ward's case, they decided to investigate an individual in the hope of finding a crime with which he could be charged. Ward was identified as a guilty man; the only problem was finding the right charges.

It has to be acknowledged that the police approached their task with, depending on your viewpoint, commendable enthusiasm or grossly excessive zeal. Judging by the resources thrown at the Ward investigation, they treated him as though he were a master criminal who carried out the most heinous crimes of the century.

It appears that no less than 140 potential witnesses were interviewed; Christine Keeler was interviewed at least 24 times in order to drum up some evidence against Ward. In the early 1960s, the police were free to conduct interviews without any form of recording to verify the accuracy of what was reported. We therefore have no record of what the police promised some witnesses or what threats were made against other witnesses in order to secure their 'co-operation' in the case against Ward.

It is alleged, and I think probably no longer contested, that certain prostitutes were threatened by the police in terms of having their children or other young relatives put into care unless they gave the police what they wanted to hear about Ward.

On purpose or by 'accident', the police also created serious financial problems for Stephen Ward by going repeatedly to his clinic and asking his patients a series of personal questions, including whether they had attended 'sex parties' held by Ward. Unsurprisingly, Ward's patients simply stopped attending his clinic and Ward's principal source of income dried up.

Four days after Profumo's resignation, Stephen Ward, to his amazement and horror, was arrested and, on the 8th of June, 1963, charged with a variety of sex-related offences including living off immoral earnings. Why a successful osteopath and artist would need to do this has never been properly explained.

THE TRIAL OF STEPHEN WARD

It is, I believe, almost self-evident that the Home Secretary and the Metropolitan Police set out 'to get' Stephen Ward. It seems that Ward was shocked to be charged but was, initially at least, very confident that he would be exonerated. In his mind, he had committed no offence and he was incredulous that anyone else might think otherwise. He believed he had a host of powerful and influential friends who would be ready and able to put an end to this nonsense. He was sadly mistaken.

Instead, Ward was, as Americans sometimes say, 'railroaded'. Or to use English slang, he was 'stitched up' by false testimony, by police intimidation, by media lies, by the cowardice of his so-called friends and by insidious judicial collusion and conspiracy. By the time Ward realised how the dice were loaded against him, he was helpless and in despair. Suicide may have looked like an attractive option.

The key witnesses were Keeler and Rice-Davies, and both had been subject to intense police pressure. Both had few illusions about the willingness of the police to pursue them on a variety of pretexts. The teenage Mandy Rice-Davies had already experienced a stay in Holloway Prison on a trumped-up minor charge where bail was set at a ridiculously high level. In short, it was made clear to the young women that their lives would be a great deal easier and have much less hassle if they 'co-operated' with the police.

The highlight of the committal proceedings was, of course, Rice-Davies' reply under cross-examination. The prosecutor put it to her that Lord Astor had denied sleeping with her, even though it appeared that he was paying her rent at the time. Mandy Rice-Davies replied, 'Well, he would, wouldn't he?' This response can now be found in the Oxford Dictionary of Quotations and has become a regular feature of common speech when we doubt someone's protestations of innocence.

One problem for Ward was that politicians and media had prejudiced a fair trial by frequently referring to Keeler and Rice-Davies as prostitutes, and some of the charges against Ward rested on that assumption. Another problem was that parliamentary debates referred to Ward as a Soviet spy. In short, not only was Ward's reputation trashed before the trial began but so too were the characters of Keeler and Rice-Davies.

Lord Goodman, the eminent solicitor and advisor to Harold Wilson, remarked that 'I do not know of any prosecution more outrageous than this one or where there was a more deliberate and wicked attempt to victimise the accused' (Robertson, p180). The distinguished journalist Bernard Levin wrote this was 'a miserable miscarriage of justice' based on 'obviously perjured evidence'.

Geoffrey Robertson's forensic legal analysis in his book, *Stephen Ward is Innocent, OK?* is hard to improve on and I heartily recommend it to anyone who wants to know the full details of how Ward was 'stitched-up' by the British judicial system. In his study, he makes some devastating accusations against our masters, including charging the Lord Chief Justice and two fellow Appeal judges of arranging things so that 'the evidence which should have secured his acquittal would be hidden from the jury' and claiming that the trial judge 'misdirected' the jury 'in a way that led to his conviction on counts of which he was palpably innocent' (Robertson, p.x).

Without going into the fine detail, Robertson has managed to find no less than 12 grounds on which Ward's convictions were 'unsafe'. These include the following;

- The non-disclosure of Keeler's perjury in another trial
- The trial judge's grievous error in speculating about Ward's friends
- The failure to give any warning about the need for corroborative evidence
- The failure to give proper 'good character' direction to

the jury
- The judge's failure to interpret the law on prostitute's earnings correctly
- The failure to note the 'insufficiency' of the evidence
- Failure to appreciate that Ward lacked 'a guilty mind'
- The judge's decision to continue the trial even though Ward was in a coma
- And the legally improper instigation of a prosecution by the Home Secretary

In case there is any doubt about the 'dirty tricks' in the Ward case, we should also note that the Lord Chief Justice refused, without giving any reasons, requests for access to the trial transcript. And in 2011, it was confirmed that the trial transcript would remain inaccessible until 2046 - 82 years after the trial. This is the only trial in British legal history which is subject to this enforced secrecy. Is it just possible that 'the Establishment' have something to hide?

The remarks of the judge to the effect that Ward had been abandoned by his 'friends' seemed to have had a devastating impact on the defendant. The fact that the remarks were legally questionable is one thing, but they betrayed a wider truth. Ward was shocked when he was charged with pimping and other offences, partly because he saw himself as innocent and partly because he thought his 'friends' among the 'great and the good' would protect him, would rush to his side, would stand up and be counted as true friends would. But, in reality, they all ran for the hills.

There was, apparently, a meeting of his 'friends' at a London club to discuss supporting Ward but, when it was pointed out that his closest friend, Lord Astor, had suddenly found urgent business in New York and fled the country, their desire to stay, testify and accept the public and media opprobrium evaporated and Ward was 'cut adrift', left to 'twist in the wind'. It was this rejection which seemed to trigger his despair and was the catalyst for the suicide attempt.

If indeed it was suicide; some conspiracy theorists tend to the view that the security services, having earlier washed their hands of Ward, later determined to 'clean up' the situation by helping Stephen Ward into the next world. I do not know of any compelling evidence to support this, but it is obviously the case that, had Ward lived, he had a lot to reveal about the most famous people in the country, and it might well be considered in the 'national interest' to prevent a series of lurid disclosures which could compromise the highest in the land.

Stephen Ward was subject to a politically motivated prosecution at the instigation of the Home Secretary. He has been likened to a 'British Dreyfus', trapped in a situation where the legal processes were manipulated to destroy him. He was a 'scapegoat', a 'patsy', a man who was sacrificed on the altar of public, political and media opinion. Ward was, to the Establishment hypocrites, a 'thoroughly filthy fellow' and Lord Denning even called him 'the most evil man he had ever met', which suggests to me that Denning did not get out very much!

OUTCOMES AND CONSEQUENCES

Stephen Ward
The day after he lapsed into a coma, Ward died. His funeral in August 1963 attracted only six mourners, including his brothers and solicitor. There was a wreath of 100 white carnations sent by Kenneth Tynan inscribed 'To Stephen Ward, Victim of Hypocrisy'.

Lord (Bill) Astor
Died in 1966 having suffered a major heart attack in 1964.

John (Jack) Profumo
Withdrew from public life and his wife stood by him. He became heavily involved in doing charitable works for Toynbee Hall. He was eventually rehabilitated into high society and was honoured by the Queen for his services to charity. He died in 2006 at the age of 91.

Yevgeny (Eugene) Ivanov
Recalled to the Soviet Union in December 1962, just before the Profumo scandal hit the newspapers .He received no credit or recognition for any supposed spy activity in the UK. His wife left him and he engaged in a lot of heavy drinking. He died in 1994 aged 68.

Christine Keeler
Received large payments from newspapers, but found it hard to hold onto much of the money, partly through her poor judgment of men. She was prosecuted, convicted and sentenced to 9 months in prison for her perjury in the Lucky Gordon case. She was mercilessly attacked in the popular press, for example, *The People on the 4th of August, 1963* carried the front-page headline, 'KEELER, THE SHAMELESS SLUT'.

When she was released from prison, the *Daily Sketch*

published her phone number. When she got married in 1965, she was relentlessly doorstepped by the tabloid hacks. Her later life has been chequered but she periodically contributes to unreliable memoirs and accounts of the Profumo Affair. Ward's drawings of her can be seen in the National Portrait Gallery and the chair she straddled in the iconic photograph can be found in the Victoria and Albert Museum. She now has some animosity toward Mandy Rice-Davies and is devoted to her cats. She will be 72 in 2014.

Aloysius (Lucky) Gordon
Made a not hugely successful living as a jazz pianist and singer. He first met Edgecombe in a shebeen (an illegal drinking den) and later needed 17 facial stitches after Edgecombe attacked him over Keeler.

Johnny Edgecombe
Sentenced to 7 years for the shooting incident outside Ward's flat. He made a living through jazz promotion and allegedly through drug dealing. He died in 2010 aged 77.

Lord Denning
His report into the Profumo Affair sold over one hundred thousand copies, but it lacked the graphic and lurid detail many readers were expecting. Denning had a reputation as 'the people's judge' but lived in rather a narrow world himself. Once President of the Lawyers' Christian Fellowship, he held strict views on all kinds of immorality. He also observed that 'it is better that some innocent men remain in jail rather than the integrity of the English judicial system be impugned'. He died in 1999 aged 100.

Cliveden House and the author
Cliveden House became a National Trust owned property, but after the Profumo Affair it was for a number of years the UK Campus of Stanford University, California.

Fresh out of university, I was offered a teaching post there as a Lecturer in British Politics. The Director advised me that I would only have to teach one day a week, on Wednesdays, because the students were often away at other times, having what he called 'a total cultural experience'. He then asked me if I was single and I replied that I was. 'Oh good,' he said, 'because I want someone young who can socialise with the students'.

At the precise moment he said the word socialise, I saw a tall, beautiful, young Californian girl wearing the skimpiest of bikinis walk past his office window on her way to the famous swimming pool. 'Socialise?' I spluttered. 'Yes, I think I could manage that!'

But having reflected on it, I decided I was a serious academic and declined the post. Puritanism 1 - Hedonism 0!

Cliveden House is now a luxury hotel where they occasionally hold 'Profumo Weekends'.

Chief Inspector Samuel Herbert
Led the investigation into Stephen Ward and for his 'strenuous, pitiless fixing of evidence' (Davenport-Hines, p340) was subsequently promoted to Superintendent. But he died of a heart attack in 1966 at the age of 48. He left a modest estate appropriate to his income, but it was subsequently discovered that he had another bank account which contained the equivalent today of half a million pounds.

Where this came from has never been conclusively demonstrated. Some think it came from an industrialist and former Labour MP, John Lewis, who wrongly believed that Ward had seduced his wife. Others suggest that perhaps it came from Clore or Savundra for keeping their names out of the case against Ward. But whichever source it was, it looks very much like a large corrupt payment.

Harold Macmillan

The Prime Minister was badly shaken by the Profumo Affair and it has been seriously suggested that he actually lapsed into a clinical depression. He had been betrayed by a fellow 'gentleman' and if you can't trust the word of a gentleman, what hope is there for the world? One of his first actions, which only emerged in April 2010, was to order MI5 to install 'bugging' devices in 10 Downing Street so that he could hear what his Cabinet colleagues were saying to each other before and after cabinet meetings.

He was also experiencing discomfort from an enlarged prostate. Convinced, wrongly, that he had cancer, Macmillan decided to resign as Prime Minister. He actually survived for another 23 years before dying in 1986 at the age of 92. His successor, Sir Alec Douglas-Home, was an inept election campaigner but still only lost the general Election of 1964 by four seats. It is reasonable to speculate that there would have been no Labour Government without the Profumo Affair and its impact on Macmillan.

Mandy Rice-Davies

Mandy is really the only character in the Profumo scandal who appears to have thrived and enjoyed a successful life afterwards. She has been a nightclub singer, an actress, a novelist, a businesswoman and has learned several languages. She has been married three times and once described her life as 'one slow descent into respectability'.

The current Lord Astor, who is David Cameron's father in law, met Mandy at the premiere of the Andrew Lloyd Webber musical about the Profumo Affair and described her as 'absolutely charming'.

Her husband, Ken Foreman, a successful businessman, once invited an old friend to join his company's board as Vice Chairman. Mandy and Ken socialised with this friend and his wife and one report even suggests they went on holiday together once. His friend's name was Denis Thatcher! So a woman involved in a scandal which helped bring down a

Conservative government ends up as friends with Denis and Maggie. Truth is indeed stranger than fiction!

We have nearly reached the end of this tale, but it is perhaps worth mentioning one curious incident. Before the opening of an exhibition of Ward's artwork organised to raise funds for his defence, a distinguish looking, silver haired gentleman offered to buy all the works featuring members of the Royal Family for cash and he took them away with him. These pictures have not been seen since. The purchaser is now generally believed to be Sir Anthony Blunt, the Keeper of the Queen's Pictures and, of course, the fourth man in the Burgess, Maclean, Philby spy ring.

Blunt was never prosecuted for his treasonable activities because he was part of the Establishment and worthy of protection. The tragedy of Stephen Ward is that he thought he had become part of the Establishment; in reality, he was only used by it, then dropped like a hot potato when the going got tough. While Blunt was protected and Profumo was rehabilitated, Stephen Ward was maliciously prosecuted and driven to taking his own life.

A lobbyist from the International Cheese Marketing Board sought an audience with the Pope. The Pope said, 'how can I help you my son.'

The lobbyist said, 'Holy Father, it is only a small request. We would like you to make a slight amendment to the Lord's Prayer so, where it now says 'give us this day our daily bread', we would like you to change it to 'give us our daily bread and cheese. In exchange and as a mark of our respect, we will donate ten million dollars to the Catholic Church.'

The Pope was apoplectic and incredulous. 'Young man, do you really think that I would change our most sacred prayer for ten million dollars?'

The lobbyist shook his head and said, 'No, but it was worth a try. Okay, Holy Father, you drive a hard bargain. We'll pay you twice what the bread people are paying you!'

4
THE LIFE AND MYSTERIOUS DEATH OF MARILYN MONROE

Who was Marilyn Monroe? She was born Norma Jeane Mortenson in 1926 -which makes her about the same age as HM the Queen. They did meet at a film premiere, but it is doubtful they had much else in common. It is also doubtful if Mr Mortenson was her father. Mortenson was her mother Gladys's second husband, although she had left him before conceiving Norma Jeane. Her biological father seems to have been one Stan Gifford, who Norma Jeane never knew and who rebuffed her attempts to make contact with him in later life.

She was known for most of her childhood as Norma Jeane Baker - Baker being the name of her Gladys's first husband - until her first marriage at the age of sixteen when she became Norma Jeane Dougherty. I hope you are keeping up!

CHILDHOOD AND UPBRINGING

To put it very mildly, Norma Jeane had an extremely difficult childhood; no father, and a mother who suffered periodically from mental illness and poverty. Severe mental illness also seems to have affected her maternal grandparents. Ironically, Gladys worked, when she could, in the movie industry as an assistant editor and the long hours meant that Norma Jeane was largely left to her own devices. Taken into care at 12 days old, she did not live with her mother until she was seven.

As Gladys's health continued to deteriorate, she was committed to various mental hospitals, and Norma Jeane spent an increasing amount of time in orphanages and foster homes. There are differing accounts of how many placements she went through, but twelve seems a fair estimate. In addition to the emotional neglect she experienced, it appears that in at least one of the foster homes, she experienced sexual abuse at the age of about eight.

A crisis occurred when, as a teenager, her then foster parents wanted to move to the East Coast for employment reasons. As she was a ward of court under eighteen, they were not allowed to take Norma Jeane out of the state of California. The options seemed limited – yet more new foster parents or a return to the orphanage. A plan was hatched which encouraged a relationship between Norma Jeane and Jim Dougherty, the son of a close neighbour. In the absence of a viable alternative, Norma Jeane married Jim Dougherty just after her sixteenth birthday to avoid going back to the orphanage.

Dougherty worked at the Lockheed factory and the man who worked at the next bench who became a good friend of both Jim and Norma Jeane was none other than the future star, Robert Mitchum.

Norma Jeane's marriage was not a huge success. Jim Dougherty was a regular, somewhat dull, guy and Norma Jeane later described those teenage married years as 'boring'. But the marriage may well have endured but for a strange decision by Jim Dougherty. As an aircraft worker, he was exempt from the draft but, without consulting Norma Jeane, he decided to give up his safe domesticity for a spell in the merchant navy.

His young teenage bride was left alone for long periods and, as she had already experienced more insecurity than she could cope with, she felt that Dougherty, like her mother, her father and her foster parents, was abandoning her.

Left to her own devices, Norma Jeane got a job in a factory in 1944. Legend has it that she was issued with a set of dungarees that were perhaps a little small for her around the breasts and bottom. When a military photographer visited to factory to take propaganda, morale raising photographs, he caught sight of Norma Jeane reaching over a piece of machinery and started taking photos of her. He suggested to her that she could make a career - and a lot more money - as a model.

Norma Jeane registered with a modelling agency and soon she was able to give up working in the factory. She became increasingly successful and, when Dougherty eventually came home, he was not best pleased with the change in his now 18-year-old wife. He could see that she had 'moved on' and was no longer content to cook his meals and play the dutiful housewife.

In 1946, a commercial photographer wanted to use Norma Jeane for a series of shampoo advertisements, but insisted it would look better if she was blonde and offered to pay for her hair to be bleached professionally. At about the same time, she made the first tentative steps toward an acting career by registering with a Hollywood talent agency. She was advised by this agency that there was no future for a young aspiring actress who was already married. In May, 1946,

Norma Jeane began divorce proceedings from her estranged husband, Jim Dougherty.

WELCOME TO HOLLYWOOD

To baby-boomers like me, America in general and Hollywood in particular seemed impossibly glamorous and exciting as I was growing up. Cinema going was hugely popular in the 1940s and 1950s and, especially in Technicolor, everything American looked, huge, vibrant and colourful compared with little, grey, and rainy Britain. Americans had big shiny cars with big tail fins and lots of chrome. They had refrigerators that seemed bigger than our kitchens.

Americans were tall, tanned and handsome or beautiful, and they all had very white, even teeth. Hollywood was 'tinsel town' where dreams came true and thousands of aspiring young actors and actresses flocked there to enter the movie business. Most of these bright young things discovered that what they thought was glamorous was, in fact, rather seedy. Hollywood was more sleazy, tawdry town than tinsel town. Most ended up 'parking cars and pumping gas' in the words of the song.

The giant movie studios controlled the business and were run largely by megalomaniacs with a little help from the Mafia. When the twenty-year-old Norma Jeane Baker went for her first screen test in July 1946, she had to come to terms with the reality that this was the era of the 'casting couch' and that if you wanted to get on then you were expected to be obliging to studio bosses. If you were not prepared to 'put out', there were thousands of others only too keen to do so. This placed anyone without an agent or influential friend, like Norma Jeane, in an invidious position.

Her first screen test was at Twentieth Century Fox and the casting director who saw her was none other than Ben Lyon, better known to most British people of a certain age as the star of a long running radio show in the 1950s - Life with the

Lyons- with his wife Bebe Daniels and their children Richard and Barbara.

It was Ben Lyon who advised her to change her name to something a little more glamorous than Norma Jeane Dougherty. He suggested Marilyn as a first name and a friend suggested that it should be combined with Norma Jeane's mother's maiden name, which was Monroe.

So in 1946, the newly blonde Marilyn Monroe was born, and a new career and life opened up in front of her as she signed her first contract as a Hollywood starlet. Starlets were two a penny and retained on a modest wage in the expectation that one in a hundred would go on to stardom. Sixteen years and thirty movies later, she would be dead.

The new Marilyn Monroe discovered that her first contract did not open the gates to opportunity and it was not renewed. She tested for Columbia Pictures and moved there, but once again it did not work out. Undaunted, she tried again with Fox and was taken on. At last she started getting some small parts.

The small parts were, for the most part, undemanding, and her acting skills were not put to any great test. But gradually the parts got better, as in The Asphalt Jungle and All About Eve and she began to get noticed in reviews in newspapers and magazines. Her breakthrough came in the melodrama, Niagara, where she got her first leading role as the 'femme fatale' who kills her husband on their honeymoon.

MARILYN MONROE: ARTIST AND ACTRESS

Those who have not followed her career in detail sometimes form the impression that she possessed only a small talent and relied for her success almost exclusively on tight sweaters and putting on a breathy, little girl voice. But this would be to do her a gross injustice. In my opinion, Monroe was a hugely talented actress, singer and comedienne and her untimely death at the age of only 36 robbed the world of a major artist. It would have been fascinating to see how she developed as a mature 'serious' actress.

A large part of the responsibility for the false impression of Monroe belongs to the studio contract system, which denied performers anything in the way of artistic integrity and discretion. As a contract artist, Monroe had to play the parts she was told to play, and once the persona of the dizzy blonde had proved so popular, the movie moguls and producers just wanted more of the same. To them, Monroe was the successor to Jean Harlow and, more recently, Betty Grable.

Much of Monroe's nervous energy and resources were taken up with fighting the studios by resisting the stereotypical parts offered and ultimately by walking away and setting up her own production company. In the producers' eyes, this made Monroe 'difficult' and, again, a false impression that Monroe lacked professionalism was spread. In fact, Monroe was deadly serious about her profession and devoted a lot of her time to developing her acting skills and dramatic knowledge. She certainly had aspirations to be a serious actress, but only rarely, as in her final completed film, The Misfits, did she have much opportunity to demonstrate her talent.

Nonetheless, Monroe made a series of excellent movies in the 1950s. In 1953, she starred along with Jane Russell in the classic musical Gentlemen Prefer Blondes. Although they were co-stars with equal billing, Russell was an independent and was paid $100,000 dollars compared to Monroe's $18,000 under the terms of her restricted studio contract. Marilyn protested and wistfully observed,' but I'm the blonde.' Her inimitable, sensational delivery of the musical number, Diamonds Are a Girl's Best Friend, is generally regarded one of the high points in Hollywood musical history.

In 1955, Monroe made the popular movie, The Seven Year Itch, which included the famous scene of Monroe's dress being blown up as she stood over the subway grating. The filming and refilming of this scene was used by the Director as a giant publicity stunt and attracted such crowds that New York almost came to a standstill. The dress which caused all the fuss sold at auction in 2011 for $4.6 million!

The following year, 1956, Monroe made the movie, Bus Stop, in which for the first time we begin to see what she was capable of as a serious actress. This movie gave her a first Golden Globe nomination.

By 1957, Monroe had agreed to do a movie in England which would be directed by the dominant figure in British theatre, Sir Lawrence Olivier, who would also co-star with Monroe. The story of this film is told in another film, My Week with Marilyn, which appeared in 2011. To say there was a degree of tension between Olivier and Monroe would be an understatement. Some of this conflict had to do with very different approaches to acting, and perhaps to the fact that Olivier was a control freak with a superiority complex who rather looked down on Monroe.

Olivier patronised Monroe and seemed to forget that although he was directing the film, it was actually the first film produced by Marilyn Monroe Productions, an independent company. Whatever the size of Olivier's ego, he was in fact being employed by Marilyn Monroe. In other words, Monroe was Olivier's boss and he hated it. Alec Guinness described Olivier as 'unpleasant and vindictive', while Robert Stephens said that Olivier suffered from 'paranoid jealousy' and couldn't bear not to be in charge.

Despite all the difficulties between the co-stars, the film was finished on time and under budget. And when Olivier saw the final edit he was flabbergasted. Of Monroe, who he usually referred to as a 'bitch' and a 'pain in the arse', he said, 'She gave a star performance. Marilyn Monroe was quite wonderful, the best of all of us. What do you know?'From Monroe's point of view, she not only stood up to the overbearing knight, but she earned 10% of the profits from the film and was the first Hollywood actress ever to get such a share.

In 1959, Monroe starred in the incomparable and wonderful Some Like It Hot, which was directed by Billy Wilder and co-starred Jack Lemmon and Tony Curtis. The tales of her lateness on set are legendary and she had regular conflicts with Wilder about the interpretation of her character 'Sugar' Cane. When she refused to do it Wilder's way and did it her way, he grudgingly accepted she was right. She was awarded a Golden Globe for her performance.

Monroe's last completed movie was the aptly named The Misfits, whose screenplay was written by her then husband, Arthur Miller. Monroe was in poor health throughout the shoot, which took place in the heat of the Nevada desert. The director, John Huston, was a drunk and given to going off on two or three day 'benders'. One co-star, Montgomery Clift, was a highly neurotic, repressed homosexual with a variety of psychological issues. The other was Clark Gable who liked a drink or seven himself, and who bore a striking resemblance to Stan Gifford, the man Monroe believed was her biological father. The movie was not a success at the time, but is now widely regarded as a cinema classic.

Monroe embarked on one final movie, Something's Got to Give, but it was unfinished at the time of her death. It is possible however to see some 40 minutes or so of the movie on YouTube and readers can make their own judgments about Monroe's health and wellbeing when she died.

THE ART OF ACTING

To many actors, acting is about pretending, about simulation. But that was not Monroe's approach. She studied under Lee Strasberg at the famous Actor's Studio in New York and favoured the so-called 'method' acting approach, whereby an actor has to get in touch with real feelings and authentic personal experiences, to inhabit the part, rather than simply 'pretend'.

Interestingly, when Olivier played against another modern method actor, Dustin Hoffman, in The Marathon Man, he was astonished when Hoffman told him he had been up all night in order to convey the extreme tiredness the character was supposed to be exhibiting. Olivier is reputed to have responded along the lines of, 'why don't you just try acting?'

A 'pretend' actor can switch from one role to another and go in and out of character at will. But, for a method actor, getting into character takes time and preparation and the longer it took, the more frustrating actors like Olivier found it. One biographer has observed that, for his role as Nazi dentist torturing Hoffman in The Marathon Man, Olivier didn't need to act - that is just how he was in real life!

How good an actress was Monroe? Opinions are subjective, but she was judged the 6th best female actress of all time by the American Film Institute. Her guru, Lee Strasberg once said, 'I have worked with hundreds and hundreds of actors, only two stand out way above the rest - Marlon Brando and Marilyn Monroe.'

Most professional drama coaches will tell you that comedy is much more difficult than serious drama. Marilyn Monroe was a consummate comedienne and it is not absurd to believe that she could have extended her range given the right opportunities.

She was certainly serious about developing her craft and she wanted to eclipse her rival, Elizabeth Taylor, who was not only paid much more than Monroe but who was also treated much better than Monroe was by Twentieth Century Fox. Ironically, it was Fox's problems with Taylor over the escalating costs of Cleopatra that later led to Fox sacking Monroe from Something's Got to Give. They literally couldn't afford to sustain the losses from two movies over-running and over-shooting their budgets.

Before moving to the vexed question of Monroe's death, it may be useful to say something about her relationships, marriages and health.

LOVE, MARRIAGE, HEALTH AND INSECURITIES

We have already seen that her first marriage to Jim Dougherty was something of a disappointment and scarcely a love match. It was rather a marriage of convenience which allowed her to stay out of the state orphanage. She married him in 1942 and divorced him in 1946 to pursue her Hollywood dream.

Monroe did not enjoy robust good health. She had severe nerves and stage fright which inhibited her performances, as well as causing many delays on set. Her health issues included an appendectomy, at least one abortion, two miscarriages, an ectopic pregnancy, impacted gallstones and a gall bladder operation, chronic insomnia and sinusitis.To manage these difficulties she relied, as was common in Hollywood during this period, increasingly on 'uppers' and 'downers' and quite a lot of champagne.

Her legendary lateness on set was partly due to nerves and insomnia, but also because she was Marilyn Monroe. Whereas a male co-star, if they overslept after a hard night, would just jump in the shower and then head for the studio, Monroe had an image, a special look, to maintain. So she had to summon her make-up artist and her hairdresser to make her look like 'the Goddess' because people would not accept anything less. This all took time and exacerbated her poor timekeeping.

Her second marriage took place in 1954 and her husband this time was no 'ordinary Joe' but rather Joe DiMaggio, 'jolting Joe', who was the most famous sportsman in the United States. Given that baseball is not played in the UK, it is probably worth stressing for British readers this man's fame. DiMaggio should be seen as an American David Beckham in terms of his public profile. He was a superstar. So we have the wedding of 'the Goddess' as Monroe was sometimes known to the American sporting superstar.

Their marriage was surprisingly brief, though they sustained a friendship and some kind of relationship for the rest of Monroe's life. He was besotted by her and acutely jealous. At the risk of stereotyping, DiMaggio was a typical Italian husband who basically disapproved of his wife's career, distrusted and disliked all the Hollywood people and who generally thought that Monroe should stay at home, cook his pasta and produce some 'Joe juniors'. This was not how Monroe saw her future.

Even on their honeymoon, the omens were not good. DiMaggio had a long-standing commitment to visit Japan - one of the few countries that play baseball - and while there, he and Monroe were approached by the American Ambassador. The Korean War was still in full swing and they were asked if they would visit the troops to raise morale. DiMaggio said he would be delighted but the Ambassador said, 'Sorry, I meant would Marilyn go?' DiMaggio was not best pleased, but Monroe went off to Korea and entertained tens of thousands of troops who were, shall we say, quite pleased to see her.

DiMaggio's jealousy flared up again when Monroe was shooting The Seven Year Itch and the famous scene with the dress and the subway draught was shot over and over again. DiMaggio became apoplectic, the couple had a huge row and, it is widely believed, DiMaggio hit her. Monroe divorced DiMaggio in 1955 after only 9 months of marriage. He retained his strong and protective feelings toward her and whenever she was feeling low and depressed, she would often contact him. He seemed to be the one man she could rely on when in trouble.

Monroe's third and final husband (1956-1961) was Arthur Miller, the playwright, who had some claim to being one of America's leading public intellectuals. Miller was a complex and a rather aloof and cold man. He was obsessed with his own work and Monroe increasingly felt that she was supporting him rather more than he was supporting her.

Miller relied on Monroe's income to refurbish his New York farmhouse. His determination to allow nothing to deflect him from his own priorities can be judged by his later decision to put his child, who had Down's Syndrome, into a home and then never to visit him. Monroe realised that in order to escape from his 'writer's block', Miller was basing his future work around neurotic female characters that bore a close resemblance to Marilyn Monroe. This is true of both the play After the Fall and his screenplay for the movie, The Misfits. To say that Monroe was not amused is an understatement.

Understanding other people's marriages and relationships is fraught with difficulty, but Monroe's three husbands were addressed by her as 'daddy', 'pappy' and 'papa'. It perhaps doesn't take a degree in psychiatry to suggest that her marriages were part of a quest for stability, security and, above all, a father figure.

There seems little doubt that Monroe also had a number of other relationships including with Marlon Brando, Yves Montand and Frank Sinatra. One problem in writing about her personal relationships is that, after her untimely death, a whole raft of men has emerged from the woodwork to claim that they were intimate with Monroe. I suspect that, in most of these cases, these were expressions of wishful thinking rather than actual relationships.

The relationships which create the most difficulty and which may impact the most on how we interpret Monroe's death are her relationships with President John F. Kennedy and his kid brother, Attorney-General Bobby Kennedy. It seems very likely that Monroe did have a physical relationship with the President, but it also seems likely that he regarded as not much more than another 'notch on his bedpost'.

It is also indisputable that Kennedy was a risk-taker and a number of those around him, including his brother, warned him of how reckless his behaviour was. To have casual encounters with unknown women is one thing, but to have a relationship with the most famous woman in the world, 'the Goddess', who was known to be emotionally fragile and unstable, was to invite trouble.

Equally, there is no doubt that Monroe's appearance at the birthday tribute to the President, at which she sang her notorious version of Happy Birthday while wearing that dress she had to be sown into, was organised by Bobby Kennedy. There were few people in Madison Square Garden that night that were under any illusion as to the nature of Monroe's relations with the President. Significantly, knowing of Monroe's appearance, Jackie Kennedy did not attend the birthday tribute or the party afterwards.

Some accounts suggest that Monroe was living in a fantasy world if she thought Jack Kennedy would leave his wife for her. But, from her perspective, she had already married America's most famous sportsman and America's most famous dramatist so why not the President, especially after he secured his re-election. A president can only serve two terms, so presumably Kennedy had no further political ambitions.

It seems clear that whatever the relationship between Monroe and Kennedy, it was Bobby Kennedy who was given the task of telling Marilyn that it was over and she was not to call the White House any more. Some accounts suggest, and I am inclined to agree, that Bobby Kennedy, who did not share his brother's reputation as a philanderer, also fell for Monroe. The question of Bobby's relationship with Monroe both as a possible lover and as arch defender of his brother's reputation is central to the sinister accounts of Monroe's death and we will return to it later.

THE LAST DAYS AND DEATH OF MARILYN MONROE

One central misunderstanding and misconception regarding Monroe's death is that her psychological state was very low because her career was effectively over. It is true that she was sacked by the Fox Studio from the movie Something's Got to Give in June 1962, ostensibly because she had defied them in attending the Kennedy birthday tribute. The real reasons were that the production was behind schedule and Monroe's notorious lateness and recurrent health issues were driving up costs for the near bankrupt studio. Fox was bankrupt not because of Monroe, but because of Elizabeth Taylor and Cleopatra. Monroe actually had it written into her contract that she could attend the birthday tribute.

The truth about her sacking is quite revealing because Fox imagined it would be quite easy to replace Monroe with a more pliable and reliable actress. But they reckoned without her co-star, Dean Martin, who, when told of Monroe'S sacking and replacement, refused to take any further part in the film. Martin said that he had only taken the part because he wanted to work with Monroe, so if there was no Monroe, there was no Martin. This left Fox Studios between a rock and a hard place.

Rather than Monroe's career being at its lowest ebb, the opposite is nearer the truth. Not only was she reinstated onto Something's Got to Give on the 1st of August 1962, but she negotiated two more movies of her own choosing for a combined fee of $1 million dollars - by far the most she had ever earned in her career.

A second misconception is that Monroe was facing the fact that her days as a 'sex symbol' were numbered. She was getting older and, in the words of her most famous song, was having to come to terms with the fact that 'we all lose our charms in the end'. But this is, I think, profoundly wrong; you only have to view the footage of Something's Got to Give on YoutTube to see what state Monroe was in. She looks the picture of health, clear eyed, well toned and absolutely stunning. Her long time friend and makeup artist, Allan 'Whitey' Snyder, visited her a few days before her death and said, 'she never looked better and was in great spirits'.

She spent the weekend before her death at Cal-Neva, the nightclub casino owned by Frank Sinatra and Sam Giancana, the Chicago Mafia boss. Both the owners were in attendance along with Peter Lawford and his wife Pat who was Jack Kennedy's sister, Buddy Greco, Dean Martin and others. In some accounts, Joe DiMaggio turned up and was angry with Sinatra and Giacana. Some accounts suggest that Monroe was invited, at least in part, because the Kennedys wanted to warn her off saying anything in public about her relationships with them. Greco has said that Monroe got drunk and very upset and some identify this weekend as the source of her remark that she was 'tired of being passed around like a piece of meat'. Whatever occurred, 5 days later she was dead.

CAST OF CHARACTERS IN DEATH OF MONROE

Dr Ralph Greenson; Psychiatrist
Dr Hyman Engelberg; Physician
Eunice Murray; 'Housekeeper'
Norman Jeffries; Handyman and Murray's son-in-law
Sergeant Jack Clemmons; LAPD
Peter Lawford; 'Friend' and Neighbour
John F. Kennedy; POTUS
Bobby Kennedy; Attorney-General
Pat Newcomb; Publicist And 'Friend'

TIMELINE

Marilyn Monroe's last day on earth was spent at her home in Brentwood. Part of the day was spent with her 'friend' and publicist Pat Newcomb who had stayed over the previous night. According to her, Monroe was grumpy and in a bad mood partly because she had been awake most of the night with her usual insomnia while Newcomb slept like a log and didn't get up until midday. Newcomb decided to go home in the late afternoon.

In the afternoon, Monroe was visited by her psychiatrist, Dr Ralph Greenson. This was not unusual because he saw Monroe most days. He was a well known celebrity psychiatrist who had treated Vivien Leigh and even Frank Sinatra, but it was Monroe who was his special project. His treatments were intended to reduce her dependence on sleeping pills and alcohol, so you might think not entirely successful.

His techniques were unorthodox and some say unethical. He did not seem to regard having clear boundaries between patient and doctor as important and, indeed, at one period, she stayed in his home almost as a member of his family - yet another 'father' figure for Marilyn. It is also reported that he once assured a studio executive that he could get Marilyn to do anything he wanted her to do.

Part of his control was exercised through Eunice Murray, the housekeeper, who had previously worked as a nurse for Greenson and who kept him informed about Monroe's activities. Even the handyman hired to do work on Monroe's new home turned out to be Murray's son-in-law, so Monroe was surrounded by people who were connected to her psychiatrist. Monroe did not like Murray, and had in fact given her notice to quit.

Some accounts suggest that Monroe had another visitor that evening, Bobby Kennedy, who allegedly was seeking to gain possession of a red diary or notebook Monroe was believed to have kept in case it contained incriminating information about him or his brother. It was also his purpose to ensure that Monroe understood that their affair was over and that she was not to tell anyone about it.

Significantly, Monroe had called a press conference in the following week. It is not clear why she did so, perhaps to talk about her new movies, was it to announce a possible re-marriage to DiMaggio or was it perhaps to reveal her connections with the Kennedys? Bobby Kennedy always denied being in Los Angeles that day but, as Mandy Rice-Davies so wisely observed, 'he would wouldn't he?' Years later, both the housekeeper, Murray and her son-in-law, Jeffries, claimed Bobby Kennedy was at the house that day.

A major problem in constructing a timeline is that some key information is simply not there. For example, many phone records are not available, some people have changed their stories and it is hard to find corroboration for other accounts. In particular there is a key conflict between the reports of Joe DiMaggio Jr and Peter Lawford. By the younger DiMaggio's account, he spoke to Monroe between 7.15 and 7.30pm on the 4th of August 1962, and he reports that she was on good form and in good humour. Whereas Lawford, who claimed to have spoken to her a few minutes later, reports that she was groggy, her voice slurred and that, in a later call, she told him to say 'Goodbye to the President'.

It seems improbable that both accounts can be true, given that the gap between the calls must have been very short. Who do you believe? Who could you trust?

Who was Peter Lawford? Lawford (1923-1984) was a British actor who had an unusual upbringing - he didn't go to school and wore girl's clothing until he was ten - but when he made his way to Hollywood he met and married Patricia Kennedy, the sister of the president to be. His Kennedy connections made him useful to Frank Sinatra, who took him up and made him a minor member of the 'Rat Pack'.

But to many critics, Lawford was little more than a pimp both for the Kennedys and the 'Rat Pack'. Lawford was expelled from the 'Rat Pack' by Sinatra for failing to ensure that President Kennedy stayed at Sinatra's home. Apparently, some presidential advisors were concerned about Sinatra's connections with the 'Mob' and especially his links to Sam Giancana, with whom he co-owned Cal-Neva. To exacerbate Sinatra's anger, Kennedy stayed with Bing Crosby, who was a lifelong Republican.

Peter Lawford was something of a degenerate, a notorious womaniser, boozer and drug taker. Patricia Kennedy divorced him because of his behaviour in 1966. He supposedly asked Marilyn to a meal and a party at his home that fateful last night of her life and she declined. But as Lawford's idea of such an evening was to order a Chinese takeaway and bring in some hookers, no wonder Marilyn turned him down.

The key problem is, I think, that Lawford would say or do anything to keep in the Kennedys' good books or reintegrate himself into the 'Rat Pack', and I therefore regard his overriding loyalties to Kennedy and Sinatra as making him an unreliable witness whose accounts should not be accepted without corroborating evidence.

A number of people came forward and claimed to have had phone conversations with Marilyn Monroe on that last evening, and it is difficult to know who, if anyone, to believe.

Sydney Guilaroff, her hairdresser, claims she called him twice in a hysterical state, saying that Bobby Kennedy had been at the house with Lawford and they were threatening her. Others claim her last call was to the White House.

THE INTEGRITY OF EVIDENCE AND EVIDENCE OF INTEGRITY

The room in which Marilyn Monroe supposedly died was never treated as a crime scene, presumably because the police officers accepted the suicide version given by her attending doctors. The consequence is that it is now impossible to ascertain what was there and what was not, or whether the room had been 'arranged' to suit the suicide narrative.

There are a number of key questions in establishing the proximate and indirect causes of her death.

What was the time of death?
Can anything lawford reported be relied on?
Who did she phone, who phoned her, when and why?
Was Robert Kennedy in Los Angeles that day?
How many drugs did Monroe have in her possession and who supplied them?
How many and which drugs did she consume and how?
Was she in the habit of taking enemas?
Who administered them?
Did she have a personal diary or notebook? If so, where is it?
Was her house bugged and, if so, by whom?
Why were the toxicology samples destroyed without being tested?
What was the subject of Monroe's press conference on the 7th of August?
Why is there only one photograph of Monroe with the Kennedys?

The 'official' Timeline goes a little like this:

9.30pm
Lawford calls again and asks Murray to check on Monroe. She reports all is well.

3.30am
Murray wakes, says she sees light under Monroe's bedroom

door but cannot get in or get a response. She calls the psychiatrist, Greenson.

3.40am
Greenson arrives. He goes outside and breaks the window pane to open the window. He finds Monroe not breathing, naked, face down on bed, phone in hand. He calls her physician, Engelberg.

3.50am
Engelberg arrives and declares Monroe dead.

4.25am
LAPD get a call from Monroe's house to tell them she has committed suicide.

4.30am
Sergeant Jack Clemmons arrives to check if it is a hoax. He says he was first told by Greenson, who did most of the talking, that Monroe had died at 12.30am! When asked why the delay, Greenson replied they needed permission from Fox Studios.

4.30am
Murray, the housekeeper, was washing sheets!

5.30am
Investigating police arrive and are told by doctors and Murray that time of death was 3.50am, and not the 12.30am they had initially told Clemmons.

5.40 am
Undertaker arrives. He estimated from the rigor mortis that Monroe had died sometime between 9.30 and 11.30pm, 4th of August.

Later that day, pathologist, Thomas Noguchi, records the official verdict as 'probable suicide'. There is no tick box for this and it is very unusual, so Noguchi added the 'probable' in his own handwriting.

THEORIES ABOUT THE DEATH OF MARILYN MONROE

SUICIDE

In this version, Monroe was bipolar, a manic depressive, who hit a sudden depression. Her looks were going, her movie career was in tatters and her personal life was non-existent. She had a lot of experience of taking barbiturates and sedatives, but she took enough drugs to kill several people. After a lifetime of insecurities, anxieties and relationship problems, it all got too much for her and she took her life deliberately.

ACCIDENTAL DEATH

She was taking different drugs prescribed by different doctors, and as she got sleepy, she did not realise how many or what type she had taken. In short, her death was a tragic accident caused largely by her acute insomnia.

'CRY FOR HELP'

On this account, Monroe had a history of attempting suicide through overdoses, but she had previously always told people or at least someone what she had done and so she was 'saved' on several occasions. From this perspective, she was seeking attention and emphasising her unhappiness in order to gain affection and protection. But, on this occasion, nobody came to save her. Did she expect Lawford to come after her alleged slurred phone call with him? Did someone 'encourage' her to fake her suicide and then not intervene? Was this a betrayal or simply a tragic miscalculation by 'the Goddess'?

MURDER

Conspiracy theorists favour this conclusion, but there are vigorous disagreements as to the identities of the perpetrators, the methods they employed and their motives. Sergeant Clemmons was suspicious in that he thought the bedroom had been 'arranged' and there was no sign of a glass or bottle which she would have needed to swallow a large number of tablets.

THE KENNEDYS KILLED HER OR HAD HER KILLED

There is no doubt that if Monroe had gone public at her press conference scheduled for two days later about her affairs with President Kennedy and his brother, Attorney-General Bobby Kennedy, it would have caused a huge scandal, especially given their roles as America's leading Catholics. It would have been extremely damaging, and possibly fatal, to Kennedy's re-election prospects, their marriages and to Bobby's hopes of succeeding his brother in the White House.

There can be little doubt that Jack and Bobby were mighty relieved that the unreliable, insecure Marilyn Monroe could no longer threaten them with such damaging disclosures. I am inclined to think that the motives described above are pretty powerful ones and certainly sufficient to commit murder. But it is one thing to demonstrate motive, it is another to show means and opportunity.

THE MAFIA

Sam Giancana, Chicago boss, was initially a strong supporter of the Kennedys and a business partner of Frank Sinatra. Some allege he helped secure Kennedy's presidential election victory through electoral fraud in Illinois. The Kennedy Administration had also approached Giancana through 'Operation Mongoose' to help them assassinate the Cuban leader, Fidel Castro.

Giancana had seen Monroe at Cal-Neva a few days before her death, had seen her drinking and getting a little wild. He may have concluded that she was out of control, something of a loose cannon, who was likely to 'blow the whistle' on President Kennedy and his affairs, and thought it appropriate to step in and prevent that from happening while attempting to make it look like a suicide.

Alternatively, rather than killing Monroe as a 'favour' to the Kennedys, perhaps it was almost the opposite - a threat, an attack, a 'warning'. Bobby Kennedy had begun a campaign against organised crime and his brother choosing not to stay at Sinatra's home were clear signs that the Kennedys were distancing themselves from the Mafia and threatening the liberty and profits of organised criminals such as Giancana and Roselli. Knowing of Bobby Kennedy's apparent infatuation with Marilyn, perhaps this was an attempt to implicate Bobby Kennedy in her death, or simply expose his affair with her. Or perhaps this was a different sort of 'warning shot' - don't mess with us but, if you do, see what can happen.

METHOD OF KILLING

The quantities of Nembutal and Chloral Hydrate taken by Monroe were huge. Some accounts claim that it would have been difficult to swallow so many pills, especially as Monroe was known to have an aversion to swallowing tablets. Significantly, as noted earlier, there was no sign of a glass or bottle with liquid to wash down tablets in her bedroom.

It is also claimed her stomach was free of drug traces which suggests either they were swallowed earlier than reported, or that they were administered by other means. Two scenarios are offered by the murder advocates; the 'hot shot' - an injection of a cocktail of drugs straight to the heart; alternatively, someone may have administered the drugs through an enema while Monroe was semi-conscious.

The 'housekeeper', Eunice Murray, had given Monroe enemas before and with her nursing background she certainly had the skill and experience, if not the qualifications, and she is without an obvious motive for murdering Monroe. But if she had administered the enema, it might explain why Clemmons found her doing the washing at 4.30am.

The 'hot shot' injection has been much favoured before by the Mafia where some need for discretion was required, but they could equally have been responsible for the alleged enema.

COVER-UP

However Marilyn Monroe died, whether deliberately by her own hand, by accident or as victim of murder, the whole story reeks, stinks of cover-up. But who was covering up what and why? If we return to some of the questions I posed earlier and try to answer them, we will see the scale and complexity of unravelling what actually happened to Marilyn Monroe.

What was the time of death? We don't know. It might have been 3.50am as the good doctors and Murray later told the police. It might have been 12.30am as they first told Sergeant Clemmons. Or it might have been between 9.30 and 11.30pm as suggested by the undertaker. Why did the doctors and Murray change their story? We don't know.

Can we rely on Peter Lawford's accounts? Probably not, partly because he changed it over time, adding and taking away words and because he was an inveterate liar, addict and sycophant to both the Kennedys and Sinatra.

Who did she phone, who phoned her, when and why? We don't know because the Secret Service seized the phone logs.

This suggests something sinister and something connected to the Kennedys, but there is no proof.

Was Robert Kennedy in Los Angeles that day? He says he was not, but he was in California staying near San Francisco. But witnesses, including the Mayor of Los Angeles, the Chief of Police, Eunice Murray and her son-in-law Jeffries say he was in LA. If Kennedy was lying about this, what did he have to hide? Did he go to her house, did he take her notebook, and did he threaten her? We do not know.

Was her house bugged? Almost certainly. The trouble is, there appears to be a whole crowd of 'buggers'. At least one Hollywood reporter claims to have bugged her home and it seems reasonable to assume that the Administration through the FBI would have done so - and some say the Mafia bugged her too!

What drugs did Monroe have, consume and who supplied them? Both Greenson and Engelberg were trying to get her off drugs but were simultaneously giving her large prescriptions - 50 tablets a time in Engelberg's case, although both saw her very frequently. Was she obtaining tablets from other sources? Did her doctors know? Did they identify all the 15 pill bottles strewn on her bedside table? Her doctors did not appear to know what the other was prescribing, let alone drugs from third parties, so her consumption is unknown.

Did she have enemas before? Yes, she did, but as part of a weight control colonic irrigation plan rather than to ingest large quantities of drugs. Murray had presumably administered them in her home and appeared to have an urgent need to wash the sheets at 4.30am on the 15th of August.

Did she have a red diary or notebook and, if so, what happened to it? Some people say she did, others disagree. Those who believe in its existence believe it was removed from her home, possibly by Bobby Kennedy or one of his staff, by Pat Newcomb, her publicist, who allegedly arrived at the house between Clemmons's first call and the investigative police arriving, or by Peter Lawford, who in some accounts was with Newcomb.

Why were the toxicology samples destroyed? A misunderstanding? Incompetence? To cover-up what they would reveal about her drug ingestion, the time of death etc. The pathologist, Noguchi, later said he was angry about it but was too junior at the time to make a fuss!

What was Marilyn's scheduled press conference going to cover? Perhaps to celebrate her recently signed new contracts for movies with Fox, or perhaps her victory over Fox rescinding her previous firing and instead the firing of the movie director, George Cukor, who Monroe could not abide. DiMaggio is also on record as saying he was going to ask Monroe to marry him again.

Or was it to blow the whistle on the two timing Kennedys? Because we now know of the extent of Kennedy's philandering, it is difficult to appreciate that in the male, misogynist media culture of the time, none of his extra-curricular activities were known to the American public. They were fed a carefully managed diet of Kennedy, the loyal family man and devout Catholic rather than his daily cavorting naked in the White House pool with two secretaries known to the Secret Service as 'Fiddle' and 'Faddle'!

Why is there only one photograph of Marilyn Monroe with Jack and Bobby Kennedy? Because all the others have been confiscated and suppressed. At the party after the birthday tribute on May 19th, the Secret Service went around confiscating guests' cameras and removing the film. Fortunately, one photograph survived, despite the Secret Service role in suppressing all public knowledge of the Kennedys' involvement with Monroe.

OUTCOMES AND CONSEQUENCES

Marilyn Monroe
She was buried at Westwood Memorial Cemetery. The funeral was organised by Joe DiMaggio and there were only about 30 guests. These included Dr Greenson and Eunice Murray. The Hollywood pack, including Sinatra and Lawford, were turned away at the gate.

Joe DiMaggio
He never remarried. He believed Marilyn had been destroyed by Hollywood and sent flowers every week to her grave for 20 years. He died in 1999 at the age of 84.

Dr Hyman Engelberg
He continued to have a successful career in medicine and died in 2005 aged 92.

Pat Newcomb, publicist and supposed friend of Monroe's
The day after the funeral, she flew to Hyannis port in Massachusetts, where she stayed as a guest in Robert Kennedy's house. The next week she was seen on a yacht with President Kennedy and the Lawfords. She later got a job with the United States Information Service, which was run by a good friend of Bobby Kennedy's, and she continued to socialise with the Kennedys until his death. Born in 1930 and at of the time of writing, May 2014, she was still alive.

Peter Lawford
He also flew to Hyannis port the day after the funeral. The police said they wanted to interview him and were told by his secretary that he would be away for a number of weeks. He agreed to his first police interview about the death of Marilyn Monroe on the 16th of October, 1975 - thirteen years later. Pat Lawford divorced him in 1966 and he remarried several times, with his wives getting progressively younger. He soon

became a hopeless drunk and addict, and died in 1984 at the age of 61.

Sam Giancana

The Mafia boss was exiled to Mexico, but returned to the USA and was found dead with 5 bullets in his mouth the day before testifying to the Senate Intelligence Committee in 1975.

Johnny Roselli

He was Giancana's man in Hollywood. Parts of his body were found in oil drums off Florida Coast in 1976 shortly before he was due to testify to Congress.

Dr Ralph Greenson

He seemed a broken man after death of Monroe. A once highly respected psychiatrist, he was widely criticised, even ridiculed, by professional colleagues when the details of how he treated Monroe emerged. After going into a long period of analysis, he suffered from depression, coronary illness and aphasia. He was once asked by a reporter what he knew of Monroe's death and he snapped back, 'Why don't you ask Robert Kennedy?' He died on the 24th of November 1979 at the age of 68.

Bobby Kennedy

Ironically, he was also murdered in Los Angeles in 1968, while campaigning for the presidency. His autopsy was carried out by Monroe's pathologist, Noguchi. His assassination has given rise to almost as many conspiracy theories as John F. Kennedy's murder in Dallas in 1963.

Eunice Murray

Immediately after the funeral, she embarked on a 6 month tour of Europe. It is not entirely clear who paid for this. Her accounts of the night in question have changed in detail with some startling admissions in her old age, including the fact that Monroe was still alive when 'the doctor came' (presumably Greenson).

Most spookily, she did an interview for the BBC but, when she thought the cameras had stopped rolling and the recording was over, she said, 'Why, at my age, do I have to keep covering this up?'

Why indeed Mrs Murray? Those who really know what happened to Marilyn Monroe have taken their secrets to their graves and have left the untimely death of a multi-talented star an unresolved mystery which continues to attract great public fascination over 50 years after her death.

AUTHOR'S VIEW

The destruction or withholding of evidence is widespread in this case. There are signs of cover-up everywhere and many individuals had a lot to lose if the 'truth' emerged. The death of the key witnesses makes it impossible to reach a definitive conclusion but, if I were a betting man, I would look at the doctors and Mrs Murray.

The doctors clearly botched her medication and treatment. Engelberg seems to have been distracted by his own marital separation and there was, at the very least, wholly inadequate coordination between them in prescribing for Monroe.

Greenson did not seem to know that Engelberg was still prescribing Nembutal for Monroe, and his prescription of chloral hydrate should have been an alternative treatment for Monroe's insomnia and not used in a combination of both drugs. Mrs Murray was devoted to Greenson and simply carrying out his orders, so I think the enema scenario is very likely, and that the combination and quantity of drugs killed Monroe.

The doctors' and Mrs Murray's best hope of preserving their reputations was that her death would be labelled a deliberate 'suicide' where their prescribing negligence and inappropriate treatments would not become an issue. In short, I favour the judgment that Marilyn Monroe's death was accidental but it could be seen as manslaughter by medical negligence.

How should we remember Marilyn Monroe? Perhaps it is hard to improve on the eulogy Lee Strasberg, her acting guru, delivered at her funeral;

'A warm human being, impulsive and shy, sensitive and in fear of rejection, yet ever avid for life and reaching out for fulfilment.

'In her eyes and in mine, her career was just beginning. The dream of her talent, which she had nurtured as a child, was not a mirage.

'Others were as physically beautiful as she was, but there was obviously something more in her, something that people saw and recognised in her performances and with which they identified.

'She had a luminous quality-a combination of wistfulness, radiance, yearning-to set her apart and yet made everyone wish to be a part of it, to share in the childish naiveté which was at once so shy and so vibrant.

'Now it is all at an end, I hope her death will stir sympathy and understanding for a sensitive artist and woman who brought joy and pleasure to the world.'

A group of corrupt politicians were on a 'fact-finding' mission to the Caribbean - such trips are popular with politicians, especially in the winter! Unfortunately, their mini-bus crashed and they were all killed. To their surprise, they found themselves standing outside the Pearly Gates to Heaven. After admiring the beautiful gold, jewels and craftsmanship, they decided to knock on the door and St Peter opened the gate.

They explained what had happened and who they were. St Peter said, 'We don't get many of your sort, politicians, up here. I'd better go and check with God to see if you are allowed in.'

St Peter goes to see God and explains the situation and God gets angry with him. 'St Peter, how many times must I tell you, all those who truly repent their sins are welcome in my kingdom.' He sends him back to the Pearly Gates.

A minute later, St Peter returns and says, 'I'm sorry God, but they have gone.'

'The politicians have gone?' God asks.

'No God,' says St Peter. 'Not just the politicians; the Pearly Gates have gone too!'

5
AMERICAN POLITICAL SCANDALS

When I have given this talk aboard ships, I have, because of time constraints, had to focus on just one scandal, but here I am able to set out the story of the three scandals I have researched for a number of years.

So this talk has a single, general introduction followed by a detailed discussion of three individual scandals. They are the Watergate Scandal of the 1970s, the Iran - Contra scandal of the 1980s and the Clinton - Lewinsky scandal of the 1990s.The final part will consist of some judgements about what we have learned from the three scandals. But first I would like to make some general observations about political scandals and their prevalence and prominence in American public life.

WHAT ARE SCANDALS?

The United States is 'an open society'; that is, a country which prides itself on its freedoms and the rights of all Americans to express their opinions. It is not a closed, authoritarian society where the government strictly regulates what the public may know, think and say. So scandals are, in this sense, a consequence of freedom. Rather than being seen as a political weakness, they should be seen as a mark of maturity and strength.

A scandal occurs when a politician or other public figure does something improper or even outrageous which is inappropriate to their position and the trust placed in them. The public are 'scandalised' by drunkenness, by illicit drug taking and by sexual irresponsibility. All such human behaviours are common in society but our 'office-holders' are held to a different, higher standard of behaviour. A rock star may drink to excess or snort coke without attracting too much opprobrium, but it would not be wise for a prime minister or president to do the same.

Political scandals are hard to define, classify and measure. And there is no settled way of gauging their importance although clearly some are more important than others in terms of the publicity they attract and the consequences for those involved. As I observed some years ago, some commentators see scandals as no more than 'the froth on the political cappuccino' (Williams 1998), but I have always believed they needed to be taken seriously for what they can tell us about the health of a political and social system.

Scandals are normally defined by reference to notions of disgrace and damage to reputation. Scandalous conduct is conduct which brings discredit to an office or position. A scandal becomes a political scandal when it involves politicians or public officials.

As noted above, a scandal may involve conduct which, in purely private settings, would be commonplace but, when it occurs in a public setting it can destroy careers and even bring down governments. What ordinary citizens do in their private lives and what they expect of their political leaders are not always the same. It is then not the conduct which is important but its connection to the holder of a public role, and the expectations associated with that role, which creates the possibility of political scandal.

But not all scandals relate to personal conduct. Some scandals arise in connection with the abuse of legal process and proper procedure. So a politician who is thought to have grossly exceeded his authority, embezzled funds or who has failed to correct an error or attend to a task may also be involved in a scandal. Again, it relates to expectation of a standard of conduct

Allegations of misconduct are at the root of political scandal, but that does not mean that scandal is synonymous with misconduct. The relevant tests revolve around who makes the allegations and who responds to them. Political scandal, by definition, depends on public awareness and there can be no such awareness without some means of identifying misconduct and sharing that knowledge with a wider audience. It follows that political scandals have both political and media dimensions.

Misconduct without publicity can never be a scandal because, as Moliere once observed, 'to sin in secret is not to sin at all'. If President John F. Kennedy's reckless and extensive sexual liaisons had been made known at the time there would, no doubt, have been a major political scandal. But his political opponents, as well as the press and other media, chose not to make an issue of it or give it any publicity. Thus, there was no scandal.

I will have something to say at the end of these talks about the stages of scandals but, at this point, it is simply worth pointing out that scandals may arise not only from the initial misconduct but from attempts to conceal or minimise such misconduct. The latter often proves more politically damaging and is often referred to in the popular media as the 'cover up'.

This is not to imply that scandals are whatever the media say they are or that they are simply 'invented' by the media. The combination of misconduct and the reporting of that misconduct are the basic ingredients but for 'take off' to occur, political scandals require extra ingredients, notably an attentive audience and a process of political competition.

In assessing the importance of scandals, it is not enough to consider the gravity of the alleged misconduct, because we also need to consider the breadth and depth of media coverage, the receptiveness and curiosity of the public and the roles and positions taken by particular political organisations and personalities.

Before reaching any general conclusions about American scandals, we now need to consider the 'big daddy' of modern American scandals - Watergate. This scandal has in many ways set the template and certainly provided much of the vocabulary for discussing scandals since it occurred. With many nascent scandals, lazy journalists routinely attach the word 'gate' to whatever the scandal topic is to associate it with Watergate. So what happened and why is Watergate so important?

6
THE WATERGATE SCANDAL

The origins of the Watergate Scandal are to be found in the circumstances of Nixon's election to the presidency and the psychology of Nixon himself. Richard Milhous Nixon won a narrow victory in the presidential election of 1968 and was very concerned to secure his re-election in 1972. Nixon believed that he had been robbed of the presidency in 1960 because of the dirty tricks and Mafia associations of the Kennedys. He was convinced that he was surrounded by 'enemies' and he resolved that they would not defeat Nixon again as they had in 1960. He was certainly not a man to let a grudge go 'unharboured'. He would not only harbour grudges, he would give them a regular refit.

As the Democratic Party divided over Vietnam and other liberal issues, Nixon's poll ratings rose. In the United States, politics, money and especially campaign finance follows success. Everyone likes a winner and everyone wants to be on the same side as the winner. Nixon was thought likely to be an easy winner of the 1972 election and rich donors, anxious to get in the President's good books, were more than generous in their financial contributions. The problem was that, although patchily enforced, the United States did have a number of laws and regulations which limited the largesse of these potential donors to the Nixon cause.

The issue that faced Nixon was what to do with the large amounts of cash derived from illicit financial contributions. What can you do with 'hot money'? It seems that from 1971 onwards, you could hardly open a closet or drawer in the White House without piles of cash falling out! The money had to be put to a good, if not entirely legitimate, purpose, and one solution found was the White House Special

Investigations Unit. Internally, this shadowy organisation was known as 'the Plumbers' and, essentially, they were a team of burglars! Yes, the President of the United States was employing burglars and using illegal campaign contributions to pay them.

The function of the burglars was political intelligence - both its acquisition from political opponents and to stop sensitive information escaping from the White House to the press and others who were not sympathetic to the Nixon Administration. They were called the 'Plumbers' because part of their job was stopping 'leaks'!

Nixon hated his political opponents and regarded those on the liberal wing of politics as communists and traitors. Consequently, he saw it as his duty to protect America from 'peaceniks', 'hippies', 'intellectuals' and anyone else not truly American. In September 1971, 'the Plumbers' burgled the medical offices of Daniel Ellsberg's psychiatrist on the direct orders of John Erlichman, Chief Domestic Policy Advisor to the President. Ellsberg had been involved in the leaking of the so-called Pentagon Papers to the New York Times which laid bare the basis and development of American foreign policy in South-East Asia.

By the following year with the election looming, attention turned to political intelligence gathering. A parallel body was created, The Committee to Re-elect the President with the wonderful acronym of CREEP. The new Head of Security at CREEP was James McCord, a former CIA operative. He was asked to join an operation to install listening devices in the Headquarters of the Democrat Party's National Committee. Significantly, their offices were located in the Watergate complex, which is a large development including apartments, offices and a hotel.

It seems there were actually two burglaries, but the first went undetected. On the second occasion on June 17 1972, a private security guard, Frank Wills, discovered that doors had been taped over to stay unlocked. He called the police and, when they arrived, no fewer than five burglars were caught on the premises and duly arrested. The Watergate scandal had begun.

Other than McCord, the burglars - Bernard Barker, Virgilio Gonzales, Eugene Martinez and Frank Sturgis, were a motley crew of rascals of Cuban or Miami origin. Some had been involved in the Bay of Pigs Operation and at least one, Frank Sturgis, is sometimes linked to the assassination of President John F. Kennedy.

They all shared an anti-Castro background. Even more significantly, their documents led police to the hotel opposite where they promptly arrested two very interesting characters - G. Gordon Liddy and E. Howard Hunt. Liddy was not only ex-FBI and a former member of the White House Staff, but was currently serving as Counsel to CREEP! Hunt was ex-CIA, the author of spy novels and, most revealingly, a White House Consultant.

The burglars were reticent in the extreme and divulged nothing about their motives or employers, but the arrest of Liddy and Hunt with their White House and CREEP associations, together with McCord's role at CREEP, all started to suggest that this was no ordinary burglary.

It may be helpful to have a cast of characters to refer to in this sometimes confusing tale.

CAST OF CHARACTERS

Richard Nixon; POTUS
G. Gordon Liddy; Counsel to CREEP, ex-FBI, former member of White House Staff
E.Howard Hunt; White House Consultant, ex-CIA
John Erlichman; Chief Domestic Advisor
Bob Haldeman; Nixon's Chief of Staff
James McCord; head of security at CREEP, ex-CIA
John Dean; White House Chief Legal Counsel
John Mitchell; Head of CREEP and former Attorney-General

Jeb McGruder; Deputy Head of CREEP

Richard Kleindienst; Attorney-General

Patrick Gray; Acting head of FBI and Deputy Director of CIA

Judge John Sirica; Federal District Judge of Watergate burglars

Carl Bernstein and Bob Woodward; Washington Post reporters

Mark Felt; Associate Director of FBI and probable 'DEEP THROAT'

Sam Ervin; Chair of Senate Watergate Committee

Eliot Richardson; succeeded Kleindienst as Attorney-General

Archibald Cox; Watergate Special Prosecutor

Howard Baker; Republican Vice-Chair of Senate Watergate Committee

William Ruckelshaus; Deputy Attorney-General

Robert Bork; Solicitor-General

Leon Jaworski; Cox's successor as Watergate Special Prosecutor

Gerald Ford; Nixon's Vice-President and successor as POTUS

So the scandal involved a lot of people and some complex manoeuvrings by those implicated. The first to act was Liddy, who contacted McGruder and Mitchell to alert them to their predicament and to ask them what they were going to do to get them off. He also contacted Kleindienst, asking him to intervene and urging that McCord be released from custody before his identity and background became fully known. Kleindienst refused to become involved.

Nixon's Press Secretary, Ron Ziegler, was asked at a press conference about the involvement of Hunt, a White House employee, in the Watergate break-in. He dismissed it as a 'third rate burglary' not worthy of attention in a presidential press conference. Ziegler was an unusual candidate for Press Secretary in that one of his earlier career highlights was as a guide at Disneyland; I suppose he was used working in a land of 'make-believe'. But the police and Justice Department investigators gradually realised that the burglary was connected to Nixon's re-election campaign and, through Hunt, it was potentially also linked to the White House.

In the White House, the potential danger from the detection and arrest of the 'Plumbers Unit' in action in an actual burglary of the Democratic National Committee's offices was quickly recognised. It was time to begin the cover-up.

John Dean, White House Chief Legal Counsel, was appointed damage control officer, and he began making secret payments from the campaign slush funds to the burglars' families to ensure their silence. Their offence was a relatively minor one. A break-in of an office building with no damage, no violence and nothing stolen suggested sentences would be light. It was important, though, to assure the burglars that their families would be properly provided for until their trial and for the duration of the likely short prison sentences.

Just six days after the burglary of the Watergate Complex on the 23rd of June, Haldeman, Nixon's Chief of Staff, discussed the problems of the trial and providing for the burglars with President Nixon. They also discussed how to stop the responsibility spreading upwards from the burglars toward White House and CREEP officials. Haldeman suggested to Gray that he should say that the FBI had stumbled into a CIA operation and because of the need to protect national security, the Justice Department should not investigate anyone beyond those already arrested. Gray actively cooperated with Dean.

On the 29th of August 1972, Nixon stated that nobody in his Administration was involved in the Watergate burglary. He blamed it on excessive enthusiasm and went on to add that where overzealous campaigning was concerned, 'what really hurts is if you try to cover it up'.

He declared that Dean had carried out a complete investigation for him, so that was why he could assert the absence of any White House involvement. When he heard those words, it seemed to dawn on Dean that, as he was de facto in charge of the cover-up, he was also likely to be the prime candidate for the 'patsy', 'the fall guy' if the containment failed for any reason.

Four of the burglars pleaded guilty as well as Hunt. But the Judge, John Sirica, decided to postpone sentence because he said the defendants had not been forthcoming as to their employers or their motivations in carrying out the burglary. In short, they were withholding evidence, and he hoped the delay in custody while awaiting sentencing would encourage at least some of them to be more forthcoming.

When James McCord came into court, he was recognised by some local police, and when asked his occupation he replied security consultant and ex-CIA operative. At the back of the courtroom sat a very young and inexperienced 'cub' reporter for the Washington Post, Bob Woodward (and no, he doesn't look like Robert Redford, who played him in the movie). He may have been green, but Woodward realised straight away that this was no 'third rate burglary', but a crime which could have serious political dimensions and repercussions.

Woodward had some difficulty in getting editorial support for investigating the background to the story, but was eventually paired with Carl Bernstein, and, despite the relative lack of interest from other newspapers, these two young reporters were to become journalistic role models, rewriting the rules of investigative journalism in the United States and arguably across the western world.

Watergate investigations, criminal, journalistic and judicial, continued under the radar, but in November 1972, Richard M. Nixon was re-elected President of the United States by a huge landslide. His anxieties and paranoia about his re-election were completely misplaced as he utterly destroyed his

Democratic opponent, George McGovern.

But by the time Congress reconvened in January, 1973, things moved on. The Senate had a clear Democratic majority and decided to create a Committee on Presidential Campaign Activities under the Chairmanship of the Southern Senator, Sam Ervin. This Committee's hearings were to turn Ervin into a national celebrity and media star. His white suit reinforced his image as a Southern gentleman, as 'Mr Clean', and allowed people to forget about his racist past. At first, it was hard to find colleagues who wanted to join the committee because they feared the wrath of a very popular, newly re-elected President, and because Watergate had yet to really gain traction with the public or in the media outside the Washington Post.

The deadlock was broken by Judge John Sirica who, having found the burglars, Liddy and McCord guilty, lived up to his nickname, 'Maximum John'. He pronounced the most draconian sentences of 40 years for the burglars and twenty years for Liddy. He added that these were 'provisional sentences' and would be reviewed subject to review in the light of the convicted individuals cooperation with the Senate Committee. Sirica was not a great jurist. In fact, his judgements were frequently subjected to successful appeal but his 'over the top' provisional sentences did the trick.

Burglars who were reconciled to spending a few months in prison and willing to keep their mouths shut as long as their families were being looked after were thrown into a blind panic at the prospect of long prison sentences. McCord now wrote to Judge Sirica telling him that political pressure had been placed on the defendants, that they had all perjured themselves and that, whatever the Watergate burglary was, it was certainly not a CIA operation. McCord went further by writing to Sam Dash, the Chief Counsel to the Ervin Committee, telling him of the involvement of his bosses at CREEP, Mitchell and McGruder, as well as pointing the finger at John Dean as involved in the cover-up.

The scandal storm clouds were brewing nicely and thunder struck when Patrick Gray at his Senate confirmation hearings to be made permanent Director of the FBI astonished the members of the Senate Judiciary Committee by revealing that he had given John Dean, the White House Chief Counsel, full access to the FBI's investigation of the Watergate affair. This obviously sabotaged completely his prospects of being confirmed in the post, and when Nixon's closest advisors discussed whether Gray could be saved, Erlichman, in a memorable Watergate phrase, advised Dean to let Gray 'hang there, let him twist slowly, slowly in the wind'. Who wouldn't like a supportive colleague like John Erlichman?

It is seems that the main source of information about Watergate which was being drip fed to the Post journalists, Woodward and Bernstein, came from Mark Felt, Associate FBI Director, who, no pun intended, felt he had been passed over for the top job in the FBI in favour of Gray. But whatever the motivations of the burglars and Felt, the wheels of the cover-up were coming off. What the White House needed now was a 'cover-up of the cover-up'.

But John Dean, the implementer of the original cover-up, the 'bagman' to the burglars, started making urgent and secret plans for his own survival. He offered a 'plea bargain' to the Department of Justice and, unbeknownst to him, so did McGruder. Part of their pleas involved implicating the President's closest advisors, Erlichman and Haldeman. This put Nixon between 'a rock and a hard place'. If Dean got immunity, he could bring down his presidency. If he didn't, he would still try to implicate as many others as possible, including Nixon. Nixon's judgment was that he could still hold out the carrot of a presidential pardon for Dean to keep him in line. But it was too late, because Dean was cooperating with the Ervin Committee. The genie was out of the bottle and could not be stuffed back in.

In a sensational statement in April 1973, which really got the nation's full attention, Nixon sacked his Chief Counsel,

John Dean, and then announced that he had reluctantly accepted the resignations of Haldeman, Erlichman and Kleindienst. He referred to the 'Prussian Guard' of Haldeman and Erlichman as 'two of the finest public servants he had ever worked with'. The Watergate Scandal had not only reached the White House, it was wrecking the place. Memorably, in justifying the sacking of Dean, Nixon had the effrontery to claim on national television, 'there can be no whitewash in the White House'.

The problem for Nixon now was that Gray's collusion with Dean meant there was no confidence in the Justice Department to investigate Watergate fairly. He found himself under pressure to appoint a special prosecutor who would be independent of the Justice Department. Nixon had little choice, but he was shocked by the choice of Congress, Archibald Cox, a liberal Harvard Professor and a former Solicitor-General under his arch-enemy, Kennedy. Nixon was further taken aback when his choice of a new Attorney-General, Eliot Richardson, signalled that he was minded to grant Cox wide discretion to investigate the scandal.

Attention now switched back to Congress because Cox's appointment delayed potential prosecutions and left the field open to the Senate Watergate Committee and its promised 'star' witness, Nixon's former chief legal counsel, John Dean. Speculation was intense as to what Dean would disclose and allege. Would he take on the President of the United States?

His interrogation created the opportunity for Republican Vice-Chair, Howard Baker to ask the killer question, the one that is asked in every presidential scandal since: 'What did the President know and when did he know it?'

Dean proved to be a fluent and persuasive witness with a remarkably sharp memory of events and statements. All of his evidence was damaging to Nixon, but it essentially remained his word against that of the President. The Committee needed corroboration and confirmation from an unimpeachable source - and they found it by accident.

A relatively junior White House aide, Alexander Butterfield, was giving evidence in July 1973, when he revealed to a stunned Committee that Nixon had put in place a comprehensive taping system in the Oval Office which recorded all conversations. To see whether Dean's claims or Nixon's denials were true, all you had to do was listen to the tapes.

The Watergate Committee and the Special Prosecutor, Archibald Cox, both asked for the tapes. Knowing they were incriminating, Nixon refused, citing the doctrine of 'executive privilege' and thereby asserting that conversations with the President of the United States are highly confidential and can only be disclosed by the President himself if he judges it to be in the national interest. Nixon argued that government would become impossible if the President and his closest advisors were not allowed to keep their confidential conversations secret.

The 'battle for the tapes' was the final battle in the Watergate Scandal. Nixon realised that Cox was not going to back down and, in the circumstances, he had to be destroyed. Nixon's first gambit was to agree to release selected portions of the tapes to a special panel of trustworthy supporters, but Cox simply asserted the President was defying the legal, constitutional, process and making up his own rules. Nixon then directly ordered Cox to stop seeking the tapes. What would Nixon do to escape this impasse?

Nixon summoned his Attorney-General, Eliot Richardson, and told him the situation was intolerable. He was being defied by the Special Prosecutor and so he ordered Richardson to sack Cox. To Nixon's consternation, Richardson refused to sack Cox, but then promptly tendered his resignation as Attorney-General. Nixon then summoned Deputy Attorney-General, William Ruckleshaus, and told him to sack Cox. In what was becoming a pattern, Ruckleshaus, refused to sack Cox and offered his resignation.

The President was running out of federal legal officers and

his last hope was Solicitor-General, Robert Bork, who agreed, on constitutional grounds, that someone had to sack Cox and implemented the presidential order. The double resignations of the nation's law officers on one evening have gone down in American history as the 'Saturday Night Massacre'.

The Nixon administration was in disarray. The president had lost his most trusted advisors; he had lost his law officers and, more pressingly, he had lost support in Congress where even Republicans were coming to the view that the President had quite a lot to hide. For only the second time in American history, motions for impeachment were referred to the House Judiciary Committee.

A new Special Prosecutor, Leon Jaworski, was appointed, but he showed no less inclination to pursue the tapes than did Cox. Eventually, some tapes were handed over and one of them appeared to have an 18 minute erasure which did not appear to have been done accidentally. Nixon still stonewalled, and the case for the release of the remaining tapes ended up before the highest court in the land, the Supreme Court. The end of the Watergate Scandal was in sight.

In a crushing decision by 8 votes to nil, the Supreme Court ruled against Nixon and ordered the release of the tapes. The tape of the 23rd June 1972, days after the burglary, became known as 'the smoking gun' which clearly demonstrated Nixon's early knowledge of the break-in and his active role in the 'cover-up'. Impeachment deliberations had begun in January 1974 and ended in July. By then, Nixon had been abandoned by virtually all his allies in Congress and impeachment looked inevitable.

On the 9th August 1974, Richard M. Nixon, the man who had won a landslide of 49 of the 50 states in the presidential election only two years earlier, became the first and only American president to resign the Presidency. It looked briefly if Nixon would face a variety of charges relating to the obstruction of justice with the prospect of a lengthy period of imprisonment but, on the 8th September 1974, his successor as President, Gerald Ford, granted Nixon 'a full pardon for all offenses against the United States'. The Watergate Scandal was over.

OUTCOMES AND CONSEQUENCES

Watergate set several precedents and shaped the ways in which later scandals evolved. From Watergate, journalists learned that investigative journalism could be the road to fame and fortune as it was for Woodward and Bernstein. Politicians learned that 'taking on' a president was possible and that congressional committees of inquiry gave lots of media opportunities for 'grandstanding' by publicity hungry members of Congress.

In political terms, the Watergate Scandal was a defeat, a humiliation for the Republicans who were resentful and determined one day to get their revenge. In their eyes, driving Nixon from office for what were no more than campaign excesses was tantamount to a coup d'etat, an overthrow of a democratically elected leader by a coterie of liberal journalists and politicians who achieved by their plotting what they had been denied by the ballot box. Again, Republicans would not forget.

Nixon certainly did not invent 'electoral dirty tricks', though he was a master of them. But so too were Lyndon Johnson and Jack Kennedy.

Richard Nixon
Died in 1994 aged 81. Only in his Frost interview did he admit responsibility for Watergate.

John Dean
Nixon's nemesis is 76 and enjoyed a career as an investment banker after serving only 4 months for his part in the scandal.

Jeb McGruder
First to plea bargain, he served 7 months in prison and later became a Presbyterian Minister and died in 2014 aged 79.

H.R.Haldeman
Served 18 months in prison and died in 1993 aged 67 after refusing medical treatment as a Christian Scientist.

John Erlichman
Served 18 months in prison and died in 1999 aged 73. He remained bitter that Nixon did not give him immunity or a pardon.

John Mitchell
Died in 1988 aged 75. He served 19 months in prison.

G. Gordon Liddy
Now aged 83, he was originally sentenced to 20 years which was commuted by President Carter to 8 years; he ultimately served 4 and a half years. Wrote a best-selling autobiography and was a 'shock jock' on a radio talk show for ten years.

E. Howard Hunt
Died in 2007 aged 88. He served 33 months in prison for Watergate. He is frequently linked to the assassination of President John F. Kennedy and supposedly made a death bed confession.

A beggar in India was telling a fellow beggar that once a week he ate in one of the best and most expensive restaurants in Delhi. An average meal in these restaurants costs over 2000 rupees, but the beggar said he normally only paid about 100 rupees.

'How do you manage that?' the second beggar inquired.

'Well, I usually order the most expensive dishes on the menu and I manage to get through seven or eight courses before I'm full to bursting. And when I'm sure I couldn't possibly eat another thing for a week, I tell the manager I have no money and I can't pay.'

The manager calls the police who come and arrest me but, before they take me off to the police station, I give the policeman 100 rupees as a bribe and they let me go and everyone's happy. And the next week I choose another restaurant!'

7
THE IRAN-CONTRA SCANDAL

This is a relatively little-known scandal, but in some respects it is the most serious of those examined in this book. The scandal unfolded in the 1980s and, just as in Watergate, it centred on the conduct of the President and his regard - or disregard - for the laws and constitution of the United States. Nixon's successor, Gerald Ford, the man who reputedly was unable to 'walk and chew gum at the same time', was defeated in the 1976 presidential election by the Democrat, Jimmy Carter. Carter had no experience or background in foreign affairs, but toward the end of his first and only term in the White House, he ran into some particularly difficult and intractable issues. His inability to resolve these issues before leaving the White House laid the groundwork for the Iran-Contra Scandal.

1979 was an especially bad year for American foreign policy in that it saw the overthrow of the Shah of Iran, who had been a particular 'friend' of the United States, and his replacement by a theocratic, virulently anti-Western regime. Relations were further exacerbated by Carter's decision to allow the Shah into the United States to receive treatment for his cancer. From the point of view of Ayatollah Khomeini, the Americans were giving shelter to their arch enemy. This led directly to the invasion of the American Embassy in Tehran and the seizure of 52 American citizens as hostages by the Iranian revolutionaries.

Also in 1979, a revolutionary group known as the Sandinistas carried out a revolution in Nicaragua and this compounded American fears of another Cuban-style revolutionary government in America's backyard. In central and southern America, successive American Administrations had a record of supporting dictatorial and repressive regimes in the hope and expectation of holding back the tides of communism.

Carter's inability to free the hostages in Iran and his equal inability to control events in Central America both contributed to his defeat in the presidential election of 1980 at the hands of the Republican, Ronald Reagan. A former state governor like Carter, Reagan had little knowledge of foreign policy beyond the instinct that somehow the United States needed to 'stand up' against the forces of international terrorism.

Reagan was determined that his Administration could not be characterised by the same passivity that seemed to afflict the Carter Administration. Carter was a much more thoughtful man and his inaction was driven largely by his appreciation of the complexities of the problems he faced and the inadequacy of the foreign policy tools at his disposal. Reagan, on the other hand, was less troubled by uncertainty and was resolved to 'do something'.

His first decision was to oppose the Sandinista revolution and its government. Reagan ordered the CIA to give material support, training, logistical help and weapons to a motley group of Nicaraguan rebels who opposed the revolution. The label attached to these disparate elements was 'the contras 'in that they were against the Sandinista Government in Managua and they were aided in launching a guerrilla war.

One key problem for the Reagan Administration in both Iran and Nicaragua is that foreign policy design and regulation is shared, under the American Constitution, between the President and Congress. And there were already in existence a number of congressional resolutions designed to prevent the United States being sucked into a war in either Central America or the Middle East. It was, for example, forbidden to trade with 'terrorist states' such as Iran. There were also sanctions against arming rebels overseas, such as in Nicaragua. The question for Reagan and his advisors was whether to accept the limitations imposed on his freedom of action by Congress, or whether to pursue independent presidential goals by independent presidential means.

Large foreign policy shocks kept occurring, notably the bombs in Beirut in 1983 that killed 241 American military personnel, causing much soul-searching in the White House. In addition, a fashion for kidnapping Westerners, especially in Lebanon, began to take hold. The kidnapping of Terry Waite, Brian Keenan and John McCarthy attracted huge publicity in the UK. Such high-profile cases again raised the question of what the President would do to save American hostages. What could the President do?

Long established policy and precedence dictated that there could be no negotiation with kidnappers, but the kidnapping, videoed torture and death of CIA Station Chief, William Buckley, understandably caused the President and his closest advisors great distress. The pressure to 'do something' sharply increased. Reagan felt more comfortable reacting to people rather than principles or dogmas and decided he would act.

He became convinced that it was time to try and build some bridges with Iran. The hostage taking was escalating, the influence of the Soviet Union seemed to be growing in the region and the outcome of the Iran-Iraq War was uncertain. The government of Israel, a close American ally, encouraged the Reagan Administration to secure better channels of communication with Tehran.

A startling proposal was made by National Security Advisor, Robert 'Bud' McFarlane. The government of the United States, through third parties, should agree to sell arms to the terrorist state, Iran. Clearly, any such action needed to be conducted in the utmost secret, as it was directly contrary to publicly declared American policies and principles. It was this proposal that lies at the heart of the Iran-Contra Scandal and, before considering this further, it may be useful to identify the main characters in the drama.

CAST OF CHARACTERS

Ronald Reagan; POTUS
Robert 'Bud' McFarlane; National Security Advisor
Bill Casey; Director of the CIA
George Schultze; Secretary of State
Caspar Weinberger; Secretary of Defense
John Poindexter; McFarlane's successor as National Security Advisor
Lt Col Oliver North; member of National Security Council staff
John Tower; Chairman of Presidential Commission into Iran-Contra
Lawrence Walsh; Independent Counsel investigating Iran-Contra
Senator Daniel Inouye; Chair, congressional committee investigating Iran-Contra

McFarlane's remarkable recommendation was supported by Casey and the CIA, opposed by Schultze and Weinberger, but ultimately accepted by the President. It was agreed that, working with Israeli and Iranian intermediaries, the United

States would sell arms to Iran. It was envisaged, initially at least, that the arms would be sold to Iran by their arch enemy, Israel, on the strict understanding that the Americans would then duly replenish Israeli weapons stocks. But the third party sales quickly became direct transactions, utilising a number of highly dubious individuals as intermediaries, or 'cut-outs' as they call them in the secret world of intelligence.

The implementation of this dramatic initiative was given to the staff of the National Security Council, which was in itself highly unusual. NSC staffers are generally engaged in analytic policy-related work and serve as advisors rather than implementers of policy. McFarlane chose to delegate much of the work to his deputy-director for politico-military affairs, Lt Col Oliver North, because he was a man with a 'can-do' attitude. McFarlane resigned early in Reagan's second term in December 1985, but he stayed in close contact with his successor and former deputy, Vice-Admiral John Poindexter, as well as with North.

Oliver North discharged his duties with great diligence; so much so that he brought a whole new dimension to the operation conceived by McFarlane. The sale of arms proved very profitable for the US Government, not least because the Iranians had generally been charged between two and three times the going rates for the arms. This profit margin caused Oliver North to have what he later referred to as his 'neat idea'. As the NSC staff had responsibility for both Iran and Nicaragua, why not take the profits from the Iranian arms sales and use that money to supply arms and give other support to the 'contra' rebels in Nicaragua?

Well, one reason might be that it was contrary to several congressional resolutions, but North and others saw the 'neat idea' as hitting two policy birds with one stone. As long as the Iranians did not discover they were being ripped off and as long as the support for the 'contras' remained clandestine, what could go wrong? Well, as it turned out, quite a lot.

But the primary purpose of the Iranian arms sales was not

to make profits; rather, it was to help build bridges to 'moderate' elements in Iran. This gave rise to what turned out to be probably the most bizarre diplomatic mission in the history of international diplomacy.

In May, 1986, McFarlane, North and an Israeli official, probably from Mossad, all travelled to Tehran using Irish passports! They came bearing some unusual 'presents' for the Iranian 'moderates' they expected to meet. The presents included a bible signed by President Reagan and a chocolate cake baked by a kosher baker in Tel Aviv! But when they arrived there was nobody there to meet them and had to return home, presumably with the bible and chocolate cake.

On the 2nd November 1986, the American hostage, David Jacobsen, was released in exchange for 500 missiles. But the next day, the 3rd November, the sky fell in. A Lebanese newspaper reported not only the absurd McFarlane diplomatic mission, but also exposed the sale of arms to Iran by the American government. The 'arms for hostages' operation came to a shuddering halt.

The sequence of events and decisions in Iran-Contra could not be lightly dismissed. This was no 'third rate burglary'. In Iran-Contra, the United States government had been caught selling arms to terrorists in ways directly contrary to American law and its stated principles. Furthermore, the United States government was, at the same time, illegally funding and arming a war in Central America. If Nixon could be forced from office by Watergate, would a second Republican president in a dozen years be facing impeachment, or would he be able, somehow, to survive these apparently much more serious allegations?

The scandal machinery developed during Watergate began to crank into action. Within weeks of the Lebanese revelations, John Poindexter resigned as National Security Advisor and Oliver North was dismissed. The Special Prosecutor law had been amended to the title of Independent Counsel and Lawrence Walsh was appointed to investigate

Iran-Contra.

President Reagan also appointed a Presidential Commission to investigate under the Chairmanship of former Senator, John Tower. And because they could not bear to be left out, both Houses of Congress agreed to set up a joint committee which would also investigate Iran-Contra. A reasonable reader might conclude that it was possible there were too many investigative cooks to produce a satisfactory broth. So it proved.

The Tower Commission reported in February 1987, and its general conclusion was to blame everybody except President Reagan. Whether this had anything to do with Tower's friendship with Reagan is for others to judge. It found that laws had indeed been broken, serious errors had been made, and it found there were major flaws in the making and implementation of American foreign policy.

The President's Chief of Staff, Don Regan, was identified as the person who failed to ensure an orderly policy-making process and for allowing chaos to descend on the White House. But other senior figures were not let off lightly. McFarlane, Poindexter, Casey, Schultze and Weinberger were all accused of letting President Reagan down.

But the effort to 'whitewash' Reagan was not universally accepted or supported. What became clear about Reagan's decision-making was that it was unclear. Critics of the President commented that he had a grossly inadequate and, indeed, inaccurate, grasp of policies and events. One described him as an 'inattentive, remote and confused man'. His testimony to the Tower Commission was embarrassing. Reagan initially said that he had personally authorised the initial shipments of arms to Iran. He then said categorically that he had not authorised the shipments. And finally, he confessed that he could not remember whether he had authorised them or not.

What is important here is to appreciate that Reagan represented a particular style of presidential leadership. He saw his role as defining values and setting broad directions, but everything else was left to his subordinates. It is a successful strategy in preventing the president from becoming overwhelmed by the volume and detail of his responsibilities, but the president is only as good as the people who implement his broad policies.

Readers will recall that in the Watergate scandal, the united front of the Nixon Administration crumbled in the face of potentially lengthy prison sentences. It is reported that John Dean was told that a young, blonde, white handsome man like him would face a particularly difficult time in prison resisting the advances of large, violent black men. This realisation supposedly helped concentrate his mind on negotiating lenient treatment at the expense of his loyalty to the President.

But, in Iran-Contra, different investigative bodies pursued alternative and sometimes conflicting strategies. The Independent Counsel, Walsh, refused immunity to all suspects in the hope of getting one or more to crack and then implicate others. He was eager to prosecute and therefore concerned about the possibility contamination or inadmissibility of information and evidence unearthed by presidential commissions or congressional committees.

While it had been difficult to get members to serve on the Watergate Committee, they were queuing up to join the Iran-Contra Committee. The legislators were motivated partly by a desire to expose what happened, but probably more by their desire to use the televised hearings to magnify their own importance and public status. The 'star' witness was Oliver North, and Walsh was dismayed when Congress agreed to give him immunity from prosecution.

North was a polarising figure. To those on the right, he was a valiant soldier obeying the orders of his commander in chief and exposing himself and his family to great risks in the national interest. To his critics, he was a 'cowboy' with a disregard for the constitution and due process. North appeared before Congress in full dress uniform, complete with his decorations for valour. His testimony reeked of his contempt for civilians and the machinations of politicians.

He presented himself, quite successfully, as a simple patriot who was trying to defend the United States against its enemies. He did not believe it was his place to question the legitimacy of the orders he was receiving from those higher in the chain of command, and certainly not to question the authority of the President. Where critics saw arrogance, supporters saw humility. But whatever the judgement, the inability of Congress to question in a forensic manner meant that he left Congress with his head still held high.

Unlike Watergate, there was no queue of Reagan staff seeking plea bargains. One of the potential guilty men, Bill Casey, had the bad manners to die before his role could be properly examined. Perhaps because so many had military backgrounds or connections, Reagan's men stayed loyal to their master and, where they could, they sometimes went out of their way to accept responsibility in place of the President. A cynic might add that the increased availability of immunity on offer from Congress meant that Poindexter and company could 'fall on their swords' without actually coming to much personal harm.

When the Congressional report into Iran-Contra was published, it was scathing about the way in which the Administration conducted American foreign policy. But its force was slightly weakened by the fact that it was a majority rather than a unanimous report and there was a division on party lines. Whereas Nixon had been abandoned even by close allies, Reagan still commanded loyalty from his party in Congress. Nevertheless, the Majority report was damning. It concluded that Iran-Contra was characterised by secrecy, deception and disdain for the law. To many, including the co-chair, Inouye, Iran-Contra represented 'the privatisation of America's foreign policy'.

The Independent Counsel saw he was constitutionally

outranked and had to wait for the presidential and congressional inquiries to be completed before trying to convict those involved in the illegal arms sales and transfers. He did manage to secure a number of convictions, but they were generally overturned on appeal because of legal complications arising from immunity, and the conditions under which statements were used in different proceedings.

By the time Walsh was able to submit his final report in 1994, all the principals in Iran-Contra had left the political stage. Walsh felt he had been blocked and obstructed at every turn; it is no accident that his book on the scandal is called 'Stonewall'.

The final straw was a belated effort to prosecute former Defense secretary, Weinberger, who promptly received a presidential pardon from Reagan's successor, President George H. W. Bush! The President himself had been Vice President to Reagan and, before that, he was CIA Director, but he always insisted that he was 'out of the loop' on Iran-Contra and never attended any of the crucial meetings. Of course, we all believe him.

A corrupt American politician was killed in a traffic accident and found himself standing in front of the Pearly Gates.

St Peter appears and says, 'We don't get many of your sort up here, so God has devised a special procedure. You first get to spend 12 hours in hell, then come back here and spend 12 hours in heaven. Then you get to decide where you want to spend eternity.'

The politician protested, 'Oh, I am sure I want to be in heaven,' but St Peter was unmoved. 'Look', he said, 'I don't make the rules; I just enforce them. Off you go to hell'.

The politician gets into a lift and goes down to hell. When the doors open, he steps out onto a green, beautiful golf course that looks a little like Augusta and straightaway he meets some of his old cronies he has done corrupt deals with in years gone by. He plays a few holes of golf before the Devil himself appears. He seems like a friendly chap and introduces him to some beautiful, scantily dressed young women who seem game for anything.

Afterwards, he has a couple of bottles of champagne with the Devil and they chat about the 'good old days', but then he is reminded it is time to go to heaven, so he gets back in the lift. St Peter greets him and takes him through the Pearly Gates. There, he meets lots of priests and nuns. They all start singing hymns and psalms. This goes on for hours.

When the singing stops, the politician asks, 'Is there any more excitement up here?' And St Peter replies, 'Oh yes, sometimes we take turns in reading bible passages aloud to each other.'

St Peter says, 'Now you have to decide where to spend eternity.'

The politician replies, 'Well, I don't want to cause offence to God, but I think I might fit in better in hell.' St Peter smiles and says goodbye.

The politician gets back into the lift and goes back down to hell. But this time, when the doors open, he walks out onto a bleak wasteland with a cold, biting wind blowing. He sees his old friends, but they are no longer sleek and fat but painfully thin and scavenging for food. The Devil is following them around, scourging them with a whip. When the Devil sees him, he comes over and slaps him hard across the face.

'Ouch,' cries the politician. 'I don't understand, everything was so lovely but now it has all changed! Why, why, why?'

The Devil smiles. 'I'm surprised that as a politician you don't know the answer. Before I was campaigning for your vote, but now you've voted, you're screwed!'

8
THE CLINTON-LEWINSKY SCANDAL

This scandal has its roots both in an earlier series of scandals in Arkansas involving Bill Clinton as well as in the Watergate and Iran-Contra Scandals discussed above. It is also remarkable because, in one sense, it was the first major scandal of the internet age, and thus has set a new template for modern scandals and their resolution.

In the 1970s, the Clintons returned to Arkansas so that Bill could pursue his political ambitions in his home state, but Bill had no money and Hillary was embarking on a legal career in Little Rock. They decided they needed to make some money, entering into a land speculation scheme known as Whitewater. When Clinton became Governor of Arkansas, his political enemies alleged that he was exploiting his political position to block inquiries into Whitewater.

Bill Clinton's now notorious libido was hyperactive in Arkansas and there were various scandal allegations involving the use of state troopers as chauffeurs and guards for Clinton when he was visiting one or other of his apparently many 'girl-friends'.

The Democratic Party was eager to find a Southern candidate for the presidency in an attempt to staunch the loss of Southern support following the introduction of civil rights legislation. Clinton seemed an ideal candidate. But, to most Republicans and some conservative Democrats, he represented some of the values they hated most; in their eyes, he was a pot-smoking, draft dodging, adulterous libertine.

They determined to stop him by one means or another.

As a presidential candidate, Clinton's campaign was severely damaged by a number of lurid allegations regarding his extra-marital affairs. Most notably, one Gennifer Flowers, a nightclub singer, alleged, with supporting graphic tape recordings, that she had a passionate affair with Clinton for a number of years. This encouraged Clinton's opponents to keep searching for more scandal ammunition to use against him.

Clinton decided to deal with these charges head-on by going on primetime television with Hillary by his side. He did not admit the allegations, but rather chose the circumlocution, 'I know I have caused pain in my marriage', apologising for that. His opinion poll ratings emerged unscathed and soon Clinton was President of the United States.

In his first year as President, Clinton had to deal with further potentially scandalous issues. In July 1993, the Deputy White Counsel, Vince Foster, was found dead in a Washington Park. It looked like suicide. Foster had been a law partner of Hillary's back in Little Rock and had a role in advising the Clintons about their Whitewater investments. Rumours spread on the internet that Foster was in a relationship with Hillary, and that it was not a suicide. Some alleged that Foster had been murdered and that Clinton was behind it. Soon, wilder accusations and allegations were made on the internet about Clinton. If they were true, America had a president who was a multiple murderer and international drug dealer.

When presidents get to Washington, they often repay campaign favours by steering some business or jobs toward those who helped them in their campaigns. So when an Arkansas travel company got more than its share of business from the White House Travel Office, this gave rise to allegations of cronyism. Inevitably after Watergate, this little scandal was known as Travelgate.

The apparent rash of scandals gave rise to calls for the

appointment of an Independent Counsel to investigate Whitewater, the Foster suicide and Travelgate. When it was discovered that documents relating to Whitewater had been removed from Foster's office before the police had a chance to search it, the demands grew more insistent.

The White House Legal Counsel, Bernard Nussbaum, had been involved in the Watergate inquiries and he argued strongly against the appointment of an Independent Counsel. He told Clinton that any investigation would be impossible to control and would range widely into all sorts of unrelated persons and matters. But Clinton was increasingly irritated by the fact that reporters around the world kept asking him questions about Whitewater and about Foster's suicide, so he finally agreed to the appointment. Robert Fiske, a moderate Republican, was appointed Independent Counsel in January, 1994.

But, if Clinton thought he had 'parked' the scandal issues and crises with Fiske, he was sadly mistaken. Other investigations, including a congressional one, were underway. And it was in this context and climate that one Paula Jones launched a sexual harassment law suit against Clinton in relation to his alleged behaviour in a hotel room in Little Rock in 1991, back when Clinton was Governor of Arkansas.

Although the final major scandal of the Clinton Presidency is known as the Clinton/Lewinsky scandal, it was Paula Jones who was Clinton's real nemesis. Jones had been a junior state employee working at a convention held in a Little Rock hotel when Clinton allegedly exposed himself and made improper advances toward her. She waited three years until just before the statute of limitations expired before bringing her lawsuit. And, of course, she did not have the financial means to take on the President of the United States, so it was fortunate that there were some obliging rich conservative Republicans who hated Clinton with a passion who were only too pleased to help Paula Jones.

The Clinton White House was struggling to cope with

managing several scandals at once. Several presidential staff had to resign while others were racking up large legal bills. Still others found their time was consumed in answering questions from the several inquiries. This was deeply frustrating for Clinton, because it distracted him from pursuing his political and policy agenda. But it was as nothing compared to the events of November 1994.

In the mid-term elections, and for the first time in 50 years, the Republican Party gained control of both houses of Congress. In short, the whole balance of power had shifted significantly. The President was now on the back foot and faced by an assertive, aggressive and hostile Congress. The new Republican leadership thought they had Clinton on the ropes and they were looking for the knockout blow.

Republican pressure led to Fiske not being re-appointed as Independent Counsel. He made the 'mistake' of concluding that Foster had indeed committed suicide and that there was no connection to Whitewater. He was replaced as Independent Counsel by Kenneth Starr, a much more conservative Republican who had been appointed an Appeal Court judge by Ronald Reagan. Yet another investigation found that the Clintons had been passive investors in Whitewater and were unaware of illegal conduct by others involved in the development.

Starr took to his new role with the enthusiasm of an ideological zealot. He began, in time honoured Watergate fashion, by applying pressure on those around the Clintons in the hope that they would incriminate the President or First Lady. Attention shifted from the original scandals - which had proved to be groundless - to whether there had been any orchestrated cover-up of the scandals.

Clinton was now at war with Congress and this led directly to what can only be described as a 'shut-down' of the American government as a result of this breakdown in presidential-legislative relations. This meant that thousands of federal employees stayed at home and the White House became relatively deserted. It was in this context that Clinton met a young intern in 1995. The intern was Monica Lewinsky - a graduate in political science from Lewis and Clark College in Oregon, where I was once a Visiting Professor! I hasten to add that she was after my time there. Clinton and Lewinsky formed a relationship which lasted until March 1997, and led to only the second impeachment in American history.

In 1996, Lewinsky was moved from the White House to the Pentagon because her bosses thought she was spending too much time with the President. She was distraught at her separation from Bill Clinton and was befriended in her new workplace by an older woman, Linda Tripp, who had also previously worked at the White House.

What Lewinsky did not know was that Tripp was a Republican who hated Clinton and when Tripp encouraged her to share the source of her distress, she confided in her that she was in a relationship with the President. You could call this a big mistake, because Tripp took to secretly recording her phone calls to Lewinsky, encouraged her to keep the gifts the President had given her and also told her not to dry clean the infamous 'blue dress' which was stained with presidential emissions.

Meanwhile, the Paula Jones harassment case was still proceeding. Sexual harassment is difficult to prove because normally there are only two people present; it is one person's word against another's. The main technique in prosecuting such cases is to try and establish a pattern of behaviour. If, for example, twenty women come forward independently and relate essentially the same experience with the accused, the probabilities tilt very much toward the complainant.

So Jones's lawyers were searching high and low for young women who had been in 'contact' with Clinton and asking them for depositions in which they described the President's behaviour toward them. Monica Lewinsky was one of the young women so deposed; you can see where Starr was going with this tactic.

We saw earlier how Nixon had argued unsuccessfully before the Supreme Court that executive privilege meant that the courts had no business prying into his private conversations. Clinton too had his own battle with the Supreme Court in which he argued that this sort of civil suit was a distraction from the heavy responsibilities of the presidency and should be heard only when he had left office. And, like Nixon, he lost when the Supreme Court ruled against him in May 1997. The Clintons' own legal costs were escalating and even more energy was diverted to try and raise money for a defence fund.

Starr was 'a man on a mission' and was searching for evidence of Clinton's involvement in covering up the various scandals, including the sexual harassment case. In particular, he took testimony from Clinton about Lewinsky in which the President denied any impropriety. But Starr knew that Lewinsky had lied when she earlier also denied any impropriety with Clinton, because he had heard the Tripp tapes. Lewinsky was now vulnerable to a charge of perjury, and so was under intense pressure from Starr to tell all.

November 1998, was a bad month for Clinton because Starr submitted his report to Congress. This report was like no other Independent Counsel Report in that it not only went into lurid, graphic and prurient detail about Clinton's sexual encounters with Lewinsky, but it also documented his subsequent attempts, on oath, to deny them. Despite Clinton's continued denials, 'I did not have sexual relations with that woman, Miss Lewinsky', there seemed little doubt that he had been caught lying to the Independent Counsel.

Would Clinton follow Nixon and resign the presidency? Clinton always paid close attention to public opinion polling and his political sensitivities told him two things; first, public opinion was still largely supportive of the President's performance in office and, second, the Democrats in Congress were still behind him. He determined to fight on, and it seems that many people formed the opinion that

Clinton's lapses related to his private life rather than reflected on his ability to discharge the responsibilities of the presidency.

But the conservative Republicans who controlled Congress were still determined to have their 'pound of flesh', their revenge for Watergate and Iran-Contra. They wanted to see a Democratic President on the rack for a change. So it was no surprise when, in December 1998, Clinton was impeached by Congress. But the Democratic Party stood by their man and voted against impeachment and, while the Republicans had a majority in the Senate, they did not have the two thirds majority required by the American Constitution. Bill Clinton, 'the comeback kid', had survived again - but his survival did come at a price.

The Paula Jones sexual harassment case eventually came to court and the complaint was thrown out on the grounds that the complainant was unable to demonstrate any loss, damage or suffering she had experienced as a result of the encounter. On the contrary, she had become something of a minor celebrity. But her well funded legal team gave notice of appeal and Clinton decided to settle. The Clinton legal team entered into an out of court settlement with Paula Jones, whereby they agreed to pay her the sum of $850,000 without admitting any liability or making any apology to her. This did not make Paula Jones rich, because most of the money went to pay her lawyers.

Bill Clinton's two terms as president were beset by scandals; sometimes, it seems, by a veritable tsunami of scandals. No doubt the need to deal with these scandals had a negative impact on his ability to drive forward his political agenda, which, of course, was exactly what his political opponents wanted.

I used to think that the Republicans wanted to drive Clinton from office, but I think they were happy to treat him, as one Republican put it rather graphically to me, as a 'political haemophiliac' who could be prodded with a scandal fork any time they wanted and would be left bleeding and in a weakened condition. So the Republicans may not have been able to win the presidency in 1992 or 1996, but they could ensure that the elected Democrat was unable to achieve very much because his presidency was largely consumed by dealing with scandal.

As a nice footnote, Linda Tripp, who made the secret Lewinsky tapes that did so much to trap Clinton, found herself sacked by the Clinton Administration on his last day in office in March 2001.

9

AMERICAN POLITICAL SCANDALS: CONCLUSIONS AND PROSPECTS

In these three talks about three different scandals; Watergate, Iran-Contra and Clinton/Lewinsky, we have seen some common patterns emerge, some familiar tactics employed and some predictable conclusions and consequences. Everyone now knows, it's not the crime that gets you, it is the cover-up! To cover up any misdeed usually involves one or more persons lying and, once you lie, you open yourself to charges of perjury, conspiracy and obstruction of justice. Yet politicians routinely deny allegations even when they know they are well founded and likely to emerge into the public domain. It is almost as if they cannot help themselves.

But, if Richard Nixon had 'come clean' and said yes, the burglary of the Watergate Building was a crime, and admitted it was more than excessive zeal in campaigning and promised that nothing like it would ever happen again, would he have had to resign the presidency? Certainly not! Nobody was surprised that he and his staff got up to electoral 'dirty tricks' as president because he had engaged in them throughout his career. His nickname, 'tricky Dicky', was well known and well founded. Richard Nixon was the man 'you wouldn't buy a second hand car from'. Some even argue that Kennedy won the presidency in 1960 because Nixon looked 'shifty'. Nixon, of course, was convinced that his dirty tricks were as nothing compared to the Kennedys' dirty tricks in that the family he regarded as 'the Irish mafia' had actually recruited major organised crime to support their campaign.

Watergate gave rise to a new institution called variously the Special Prosecutor, Special Counsel and finally

Independent Counsel, comprised of senior lawyers from outside the executive branch of government who were called upon to investigate possible misdeeds by a variety of executive officials up to and including the president. Although these Independent Counsels did enjoy an independence from political control, it does not mean that they were in some special sense politically neutral. In fact, it was often the case that a president found himself being investigated not just by a lawyer who supported the opposing party, but also by someone who was more on the extreme of the opposing party. The political gulf between the investigator and the investigated was then often quite broad.

A second major problem with this new institution was that the Counsel was frequently given quite a broad brief by the appointing panel. This meant that even if a president was able to deflect an initial allegation, Independent Counsel, often determined to take their investigations into new and surprising territories. The result was that, instead of investigating alleged crimes and misdeeds, the Independent Counsel were really investigating the individual, the president, to see if they could some or even any 'dirt' on him. Not only did these investigations spread out from their original targets but they also stretch back in time.

In the Clinton/Lewinsky Scandal, the Independent Counsel started by exploring the ethics of a land deal which involved Bill Clinton in the 1970s before he became Governor of Arkansas, let alone President of the United States, and he ended up investigating whether President Clinton had sought to cover-up an extra-marital relationship in the 1990s.

The Independent Counsel became a partisan weapon in the battle between Democrats and Republicans in Congress; this, over time, led to disillusionment with its usefulness. Eventually, it was agreed that they would agree to let the legislation authorizing such appointments to lapse. So, if anyone had wanted to investigate George W. Bush for any possible crimes and misdeeds - and many did - there was no available independent institution to undertake it. And, of course, the Republican controlled Senate and House had no interest in investigating their own man.

Another major impact of these political scandals has been on the mass media. Before Watergate, the dominant media form was print media and there were a limited number of news outlets who effectively defined the news agenda. Senior print journalists saw their role as keeping close to politicians in order to gain their confidence, to encourage them to share on a selective basis various titbits of exclusive news. But this style of journalism also required journalists not to expose politicians' transgressions, so characters like Jack Kennedy were able to continue their philandering around America without much fear of stories appearing in the press.

But Watergate made heroes of Woodward and Bernstein and made 'investigative journalism' not only fashionable but almost compulsory for every young journalist trying to make names for themselves. So whereas the media was once largely deferential toward the political class and grateful for the scraps thrown to them, in the post-Watergate era, the media became more challenging, increasingly seeing their role as holding politicians to account.

By the time of the Clinton/Lewinsky scandal, media technology had changed. We now had the internet, which was characterised by a lack of elite control and an increasing democratisation of news and comment. Everyone not only had an opinion, but were now able to 'broadcast' it to the world. This made it possible for anyone to post anonymous scandalous allegations about politicians and their possible misdeeds. Allegedly reputable newspapers could then pick up on some of these internet accusations and report them as 'news'. As the media diversified, it was impossible to control, and elements of it became very aggressive toward politicians in general.

It is possible to express the evolving role of the media in

canine terms. Before Watergate, the media were the lapdogs of politicians. But between Watergate and Clinton/Lewinsky, the media saw themselves more as watchdogs guarding the public interest against the evil-doing of politicians. The current state of play is one where parts of the media, especially through the internet, is not content to defend the public interest, but feels entitled to assault political reputations at will. The lapdog has become the watchdog and is now the attack dog!

These scandals have had profound political consequences in terms of individuals, parties and policies. Nixon was, of course, destroyed by Watergate, having been elected by a landslide a short time before. Reagan survived Iran-Contra, but his public reputation took a battering and his lack of intellectual grasp of what was happening in his own administration was embarrassing. Clinton survived, albeit in a weakened condition, but it could be argued that his scandals affected those who followed him.

In the presidential election of 2000, which Al Gore 'lost' in a closely fought and much disputed contest with George W. Bush, he was extremely reluctant to use Clinton in his campaign. But, whatever his numerous faults, Clinton is widely regarded as the most formidable campaigner of modern times, a man with authentic political charisma. But Gore was so worried about being tainted by the Clinton scandals that he ran his own campaign and failed to exploit Clinton's electoral appeal and enduring popularity.

Given the tightness of the election, if Gore had used Clinton more in his campaign, it might well have made the difference between winning and losing. We would then have been spared the experience of having a President George W. Bush, and perhaps there would have been no wars in Iraq or Afghanistan.

American politics have been greatly influenced by scandals and because of the USA's influence in the world that means almost every country on the planet has been affected by them.

The 'what if' questions are inviting but ultimately meaningless because Nixon did resign, Reagan did sell arms to a terrorist state and Clinton did find it difficult to pursue his political objectives. The world has been changed by political scandals, and that is why it is important to understand what they are and how they impact on our lives.

CONSPIRACY AND COVER-UP? THE KENNEDY ASSASSINATION AND 9/11

This is a unique, must-read book for anyone interested in conspiracy theories. Do you know what a conspiracy theory is? Or whether all conspiracy theories are the same? Are they nonsense created by 'crackpots' and only believed by the gullible? Or are you concerned about how reliable and authoritative the official accounts of major controversial events are? Do you think some conspiracy theories are actually true? If many people think there is compelling evidence that the Kennedy Assassination and the events of 9/11 were brought about by government conspiracies, why are conspiracy theorists dismissed as irrelevant by the mainstream mass media?

Conspiracy and Cover-Up addresses these key questions directly and is a unique, must-read book for anyone interested in conspiracy theories.

The mainstream media regularly ridicule conspiracy theories and those who believe in them. David Aaronovitch's 'Voodoo Histories' is a notorious example of this contempt. In Conspiracy and Cover-Up, Emeritus Professor Robert Williams, a leading UK social scientist, challenges and confronts these patronising critiques and clearly demonstrates how flimsy and poorly founded they are. This book offers a fresh and original defence and explanation of conspiracy theory. It explains what conspiracy theories are and what they are not. Furthermore, it exposes the weaknesses, limitations and unwarranted assumptions in the accounts of those who wish to dismiss all conspiracy theories out of hand.

Professor Williams argues that conspiracy theories are not all the same and, just like other kinds of theories, some theories are more plausible and are supported by more evidence than others. To illustrate and support his argument, the author has included case studies of two profoundly important events; the assassination of President John F. Kennedy and the attacks of 9/11 in New York and Washington. Both events have attracted much attention from conspiracy theorists but the mainstream media has been dismissive of their accounts. Professor Williams takes the reader through both events taking care to identify which are the most plausible interpretations of the mass of often conflicting evidence.

He concludes that one of these events was probably the result of a conspiracy and the other was probably not. He argues that what is crucial is that anyone seeking to understand such events keeps an open mind and uses reason and evidence, rather than abuse and ridicule, to advance their arguments.

Conspiracy and Cover-up? is available to buy as an eBook from Amazon at **http://amzn.to/1tLe4xk**.

CONSPIRACY AND COVER-UP?

CHAPTER ONE: A GUIDE TO CONSPIRACY THEORY

Conspiracy theories have never been more popular. Public interest in them seems to transcend age, gender and geography. Media companies have responded to this upsurge of interest and any night of the week you can be sure of finding one or more conspiracy-based programmes on television. This book is a guide to conspiracy theory aimed at those who want to know what conspiracy theory is and what it is not and also at those who want to sharpen their understanding of two of the most important and popular conspiracy theories, the Kennedy Assassination and the attacks of 9/11.

The Kennedy Assassination has been an event of huge interest to those interested in conspiracy theories for nearly 50 years. There is a huge literature on the subject but, for the general reader, it is arcane and inaccessible. Recent weighty volumes, such as those by Bugliosi or Waldron and Hartmann, seem closer to door-stops or ships' ballast than bedtime reading. This book aims to meet the needs of those who are not specialists and also to provide analysis and interpretation of the assassination evidence of interest to those who have read widely on this topic. The same considerations apply to the discussion of 9/11 in that few people have the time or inclination to wade through the morass of published material but would simply like to know what the key issues are and how they might be resolved one way or another.

I have written this book for two main reasons; the first and major reason is to offer a more developed account of my views on conspiracy theory, the Kennedy Assassination and 9/11, than is possible when I speak on these topics to cruise ship and other audiences. The second reason was reading

David Aaronovitch's *Voodoo Histories*. Some chapters of his book are rewarding, especially those tracing the anti-Semitic character of much conspiracy theory, but other parts grated with their dismissive statements and gratuitous abuse. They prompted me to start writing my own account in part as a corrective to what I believe to be his faults as an analyst of conspiracy theory.

This book is intended to be accessible, brief and lively but it is not a book for those who enjoy death by a thousand footnotes. I am not trying to wear my scholarship heavily by supporting it with hundreds of references or a bibliography running into dozens of pages. There is, of course, a place for such studies but I want to show the general reader a path through the dense forest of conspiracy advocacy and criticism. There are many interesting debates about highly specialised and detailed side trails in this forest but they are not my primary concern here. This is a book for those who want to understand what the strengths, scope, role and limitations of conspiracy theory are and how they shape and change our understanding of major historic political events.

Despite, or even because of, its popularity, conspiracy theory generally gets a bad press from 'quality' newspapers and the mainstream media. In most cases conspiracy theory and theorists are simply ridiculed. They are characterised as stupid, even irrational, 'cranks' and 'nutters'. From this perspective, to support a conspiracy theory is to admit to some mental illness or impairment which precludes such individuals from engaging in debate with those who regard themselves as 'rational' and as 'realists'.

But is this dismissive attitude justified? Are all conspiracy theorists gullible fools? Does supporting one or more conspiracy theories really call your sanity into question and disqualify you from debating important topics of public interest and concern?

The initial aim of this book is to examine recent critiques of conspiracy theories (and the abuse associated with such critiques) in order to establish their provenance and methodology. It questions whether the critics of conspiracy theories are as 'objective' and 'evidence-based' as they suppose themselves to be. It also questions how their ideological beliefs, their vocational roles and their assumptions about the nature of political action and public policy-making and implementation have influenced the critic's perspectives on conspiracy theory.

At this point, it is simply useful to note that recent critics of conspiracy theory, such as David Aaronovitch and Vincent Bugliosi, have a habit of lumping together all conspiracy theorists and theories together. Their condemnation is a blanket one and they do not allow or concede that there may be 'good' or 'bad' conspiracy theories or theorists because, in their view, all suffer from the same or similar structural flaws. It might further be noted that these critics do not limit themselves to the arguments or questions posed by conspiracy theorists but feel it necessary to engage in the abuse and ridicule of those who espouse views they do not accept.

The largest part of this book will present two discussions or case studies of major events which have been subjected to intense scrutiny by both 'conspiracy theorists' and 'rational realists', namely: the assassination of John F. Kennedy and the attacks of 9/11. It is, of course, not possible in a relatively brief compass to do justice to the details of these complex events and the wealth of commentary and analysis they have attracted. But my aim is more limited and what I specifically hope to show is that the 'gullible fools' may not be entirely on the conspiracy theorists side of the argument.

In the light of the two case studies, the final section of the book will revisit the critiques of conspiracy theory and match them against the evidence assembled in the case studies. This should help readers consider the respective merits of the differing accounts and explanations and reach their own judgments.

The conclusion of the book will examine the strengths, weaknesses and future role of conspiracy theories in times of increasing uncertainty in our political lives and declining trust in our leaders and institutions.

Before conspiracy theory can be defended (or attacked) it is necessary to have some understanding of the concept. Definitions are not as such, right or wrong, but rather they try to capture common usage. Suggesting a meaning is like a proposal which can be accepted or rejected. Definitions favoured by critics of a particular movement or belief may not be acceptable to supporters or believers.

For our purposes I am content to start with modern dictionary definitions, for example, Random House and Collins dictionaries.mThese reference works can be used to assemble a definition on the following lines:

A. 'A conspiracy theory is one that explains an event as being the result of a plot by Government officials or a covert group.'

This definition has the attractions of brevity and clarity. It is also a minimalist kind of definition and for those who need something further and more substantive we could develop it along these lines.

B. 'Conspiracy theorists believe that many important political events or social and economic trends are the products of plots that are largely unknown to the general public.'

But it would be a mistake to think that definition B is a necessary consequence of accepting definition A. It is, of course, possible for someone to believe in a particular conspiracy theory without believing in every, or indeed any other, conspiracy theory. Critics of conspiracy theories tend to assume both that conspiracy theories are much of a muchness and that those who subscribe to any conspiracy theory are betraying some common psychological or educational failing.

The next part of this book is devoted to outlining the main lines of attack against conspiracy theory. In particular, given its recent popularity, we need to consider the contribution of David Aaronovitch's *Voodoo Histories* which has received extremely favourable reviews in the mainstream media. Reviewers have described this work as 'dazzling debunkery', as 'superbly researched...and eminently sane', 'rich and fascinating', 'intelligent and hugely enjoyable' – all this and more can be gleaned just by reading the book's dust jacket. So what does Mr Aaronovitch have to say in his apparently persuasive attack on conspiracy theory? What qualifications does he have to support his arguments? And how does he approach the task of dealing with such a diverse subject?

THE CASE AGAINST CONSPIRACY THEORY

David Aaronovitch is a successful British journalist who has been making regular contributions to the 'quality' press for almost twenty years. *Voodoo Histories* is his second book. His previous book was a travel book called *Paddling to Jerusalem*. Aaronovitch also appears frequently on television offering his opinions on a wide variety of topics.

He is something of a contrarian and achieved some notoriety as one of the few liberal left cheerleaders for the invasion of Iraq. The failure to find the supposed Weapons of Mass Destruction (WMDs) caused him a little embarrassment but he continues to offer his robust views on television and in print to all who will watch and read.

His scholarly credentials for writing a book about conspiracy theory are not immediately evident. The book is very wide ranging, dealing as it does with not only the most well known conspiracy theories such as the Kennedy

Assassination and 9/11 but also with the Protocols of the Elders of Zion, the Soviet 'show trials', the America First movement, Pearl Harbour, the death of Marilyn Monroe, the death of Princess Diana, the death of a non-celebrity, Hilda Morrell, the death of Dr David Kelly, the Holy Blood/Holy Grail debates, the Clinton scandals and, most recently, the question of Barack Obama's birth certificate.

He does not make explicit the criteria he used for selecting the particular examples except to say they 'were not chosen for their similarities but for their outward differences' (p.335). Whatever his criteria, his selection is so eclectic that Aaronovitch has, at the very least, to be very widely read. Journalists, of course, do not usually claim to be 'authorities' or 'experts' on any subject. The best journalists have a knack of being able to turn from one topic to another with facility and generate essays that intelligent readers find plausible and engaging. Aaronovitch is one of this elite group of journalists in the UK but the question has to be asked as to what lies behind this facility? What investment of research has been made to buttress such forcefully expressed opinions?

Aaronovitch has recently stated that he is 'not an expert on anything except maybe conspiracy theory' (*Times* 4/8/11). So, as a self-professed expert on conspiracy theory who has clearly read widely across different historical periods and in different countries, what does he understand by conspiracy theory and what does he find so objectionable about it?

The first clue his book supplies is his choice of definition. In Aaronovitch's view a conspiracy theory is one which involves 'the attribution of deliberate agency to something that is more likely to be accidental or unintended' (p.5). He expands the point by adding 'the attribution of secret action to one party that might far more reasonably be explained as the less covert and less complicated action of another' (p.5). In Aaronovitch's definition conspiracy theory is by definition unlikely.

To Aaronovitch, it is really quite simple: 'a conspiracy

theory is the unnecessary assumption of conspiracy when other explanations are more probable' (p.5).

Aaronovitch demonstrates some familiarity with and great enthusiasm for Ockham's Razor, the precept associated with a fourteenth century Franciscan monk, William of Ockham, who favoured ontological parsimony. The precept is often translated as 'plurality should not be posited without necessity'. Aaronovitch restates it, utilising the Skeptics Dictionary, as 'other things being equal, one hypothesis is more plausible than another if it involves fewer numbers of assumptions' and adds 'or more vulgarly, keep it simple'. (p.6)

So the reader learns that Aaronovitch likes simple explanations and dislikes the introduction of what he judges as unnecessary assumptions. His point, as I understand it, is that the obvious, straightforward interpretation of an event is likely to be superior to one which introduces both additional assumptions and complexities.

I have no special qualifications in philosophy or logic and nor does Aaronovitch appear to claim such expertise, but it should be noted that Ockham's Razor has strict limitations. It does not define the relative strengths of competing theories and indeed it may not be possible to judge the strength of different theories without the benefit of historical hindsight. It urges us to keep only the essential element of a theory and warns us against the unjustified introduction of additional elements. But my point is that the persuasive force of a theory does not reside in its complexity or simplicity as such but in its inherent ability to account for the event or phenomenon.

In any form of inquiry, it has to be conceded that, at least sometimes, a more complex hypothesis may be the correct one. Simple theories are more comprehensible and easily understood but simplicity of itself has no value if the theory is unable to explain all the features of an event or phenomenon. What I understand Ockham's Razor to imply is that 'other things being equal', the simpler explanation is to be preferred. But this begs the question that arises again and again in conspiracy debates, is the 'official' explanation more convincing, more coherent and more compelling than any other explanation? This must surely be a matter of careful weighing of evidence in each case rather than re-stating the precept of ontological parsimony.

But Aaronovitch shows only a passing interest in philosophy because he has an alternative card to play. He seems to believe that 'those who understand history develop an intuitive sense of likelihood and unlikelihood' (p.7). So, in one page, he travels from logical precepts to the delights of 'intuition' as his guiding star in coming to terms with conspiracy theory. It seems a safe assumption that David Aaronovitch is one of 'those' who have the 'intuition' and conspiracy theorists are, to his mind, definitely people who lack this 'gift'.

The dictionary-derived definition of conspiracy theory outlined earlier describes them in terms of a reliance on plots as the explanation of an event. This definition makes no *a priori* judgment about the likelihood or otherwise of such an explanation. In this sense it is neutral. But sharp eyed readers will have noted that Aaronovitch's definition depends on the notion of 'likelihood'. To repeat, he says a conspiracy theory involves 'the attribution of deliberate agency to something that is more likely to be accidental or unintended'. So it all comes down to which is more likely as an explanation of a historical event but, as he has also made clear, Aaronovitch and his ilk have an 'intuitive sense' of it. It is hard to argue with people who have an 'intuitive sense' but we ought to try.

What Aaronovitch does is to use a definitional exercise not only to identify the topic but also to evaluate it. He is concerned less with describing conspiracy theory as in condemning it. He uses Ockham's Razor to justify choosing the simple over the complex and then claims that, because plots are complicated, they are inherently unlikely.

But the judgment of likelihood is a subjective one. It is, of course, possible that all manner of everyday events have simple explanations. Someone who fails to meet an appointment may have been abducted by aliens but it is usually the case there is a more mundane explanation. But conspiracy theories generally do not focus on the everyday and commonplace but rather on the exceptional.

Aaronovitch is not putting himself in the ridiculous position of denying the reality of conspiracies. He concedes there are conspiracies but he thinks they are not terribly important or frequent. Their significance is, in his view, exaggerated and when conspiracies occur they usually fail or the plot is uncovered. He even claims that there have been very few major conspiracies in Britain and America (p.8). When challenged, the use of the term 'major' is the author's escape clause. It is not clear from his writings how much Aaronovitch knows about the formulation and implementation of American foreign policy since World War 2 but, together with many of his readers, he will be aware of the numerous American plots to overthrow or destabilise regimes in Latin and South America, South East Asia and other parts of the globe. Either Aaronovitch is extremely uninformed or he believes that a democracy covertly plotting to overthrow the governments of other countries is simply not important enough to qualify for the label 'major conspiracy'. He even seems reluctant to include Watergate!

So far in this brief examination of Aaronovitch's *Voodoo Histories* we have examined the definitional problem and seen how Aaronovitch tries to define away conspiracy theories by loading his definitions with his own judgments about how likely their explanations are. We have also seen how he invokes the precept of Ockham's Razor and how limited that device actually is. And we have learned that Aaronovitch and those who agree with him are blessed with an 'intuitive understanding' of the likelihood of certain events.

All of the above raises a number of questions but here we encounter another idiosyncrasy. Aaronovitch hates questions; or rather, he hates certain kinds of questions. To him, only some questions make sense. He believes that the asking of questions by those he regards as conspiracy theorists is meaningless because 'the questions asked, of course, only make sense if the questioner really believes there is indeed a secret conspiracy' (p.11). In much of his journalism, Aaronovitch assumes the mantle of the sceptic but, when others are sceptical of official accounts of events, he suggests the questions are in some sense illegitimate. The problem here is that, from my reading of the literature, conspiracy theorists do not experience Pauline conversions on the road to Damascus. But rather the failure, reluctance or unwillingness of official government bodies to answer perfectly reasonable questions creates a doubt in the minds of many about the authenticity, credibility and comprehensiveness of the official version of events.

A familiar line of attack from Aaronovitch is to question or even ridicule the credentials and qualifications of chose who challenge official 'explanations'. But he is not always consistent. At one point he approvingly cites French journalists who have criticised a French conspiracy theorist, Thierry Meyssan (p.12) but, on the next page of his book, he says 'conspiracy theorists are at fault for giving credence to the "passing opinions of journalists" (p.13). As Aaronovitch himself is a journalist, it is not clear how to weigh his pronouncements.

My central contention in this book is that the standing of any conspiracy theory can only be tested against the evidence available in each case. It should not be conceded that conspiracy theories can be dismissed by means of a loaded definition. From the large field of conspiracy theories I have chosen two case studies for consideration in this book – the assassination of President John F. Kennedy and the events of 9/11. These have been chosen partly because they are among the most popular of conspiracy theories and partly because Aaronovitch also considers them in his book.

But before proceeding to the case studies, we need to say a

final word about definitions so that readers will know exactly what we are discussing. If dictionary definitions are not sufficient and Aaronovitch's too loaded, the most useful starting place is to consider what scholars, rather than lexicographers or journalists have to say on the subject. In recent years, two philosophers, Brian Keeley and David Coady, have attempted to encapsulate what we mean when we use the term 'conspiracy theory'. Let us consider each in turn:

In his article, 'Of Conspiracy Theories', in the *Journal of Philosophy*, Keeley suggests that:

'A conspiracy theory is a proposed explanation of some historical event (or events) in terms of the significant causal agency of a relatively small group of persons – the conspirators acting in secret' (1999:116).

His definition is quite similar to the dictionary definition offered earlier but makes more explicit the point about 'causal agency' and also says something about secrecy and the small number of individuals involved. Presumably, Keeley believes there is a tension between these two elements in that the larger the number of individuals involved the less chance there is of keeping the plot secret. The recent *Wikileaks* controversy demonstrates, among other things, the difficulties of maintaining government secrets when millions of officials have access to the same confidential information.

In his article, 'Conspiracy Theories and Official Stories', in the *International Journal of Applied Philosophy*, David Coady develops Keeley's definition and makes some additional refinements as follows:

'A conspiracy theory is a proposed explanation of an historical event in which conspiracy (i.e. agents acting secretly in concert) has a significant causal role. Furthermore, the conspiracy postulated by the proposed explanation must be a conspiracy to bring about the historical event which it purports to explain. Finally, the proposed explanation must conflict with an 'official' explanation of the same historical event' (2003:201).

In his elaboration Coady links the conspiracy theory itself with an intention to produce a particular outcome and argues that it is always at variance with the conventional, orthodox accounts of the event.

Aaronovitch's bibliography suggests that his reading has not extended to these academic journals but presumably he would at least consider these scholarly alternatives to his own definition. As readers will have noted, neither the Keeler or Coady definitions try to smuggle into their definitions any effort to gauge the likelihood or otherwise of a conspiracy theory being true. Such judgments can only be made in specific cases after having examined the evidence and that is where we now turn.

ABOUT THE AUTHOR

Robert Williams is a former Professor of Politics at the University of Durham. Having graduated with an MPhil in Politics from Nottingham University, Robert embarked on an academic career, first at York and later at Durham. His vast knowledge within the field of corruption has taken him around the globe during his long and distinguished career, taking up positions as a Visiting Professor in the US, Canada, Australia and China.

One of the world's leading academics in his field, Robert has worked with a plethora of governments, organisations and international agencies to fight corruption, operating as an anti-corruption consultant on both sides of the Atlantic, as well as undertaking research in Eastern Europe, Africa and the Middle East.

Now retired, the corruption expert is a keen speaker, performing lectures on a wide range of topics, from historical conspiracies to modern day corruption.

He has also delved into the realm of fiction, publishing two political thrillers - The Corcovado Conspiracy and The Potomac Plot - under the pseudonym of Jack Carey.

To discover more about Robert, visit his website at **www.robert-williams.co.uk**. You can also check out his novels online at **www.jack-carey.co.uk**.

Made in the USA
Charleston, SC
26 November 2014